SEX, LOVE, AND THE PERSON

Sex, Love, and the Person

by PETER A. BERTOCCI

Borden Parker Bowne Professor of Philosophy,
Boston University

 Sheed Andrews and McMeel, Inc.
Subsidiary of Universal Press Syndicate
Kansas City

Sheed Andrews and McMeel, Inc.
6700 Squibb Road
Mission, Kansas 66202

To my brothers and sisters
Angelo, Annie, Theodore,
Mary, Jeanne,
and our children.

PREFACE

What part should sex play in a human life? This question arises over and over again in our day, and it deserves a reasoned answer. Whatever the actual changes may be in sexual behavior, there is a new ferment over sexual morality. A reasoned answer cannot be based solely on the latest questionnaire about how people are behaving—even if such sources of information were more reliable than the best of them are. For what one thinks about the place of sex is influenced by how he answers such questions as: How, in a person, is sex related to love? And what happens to sex and love if they are not part of marriage?

Today many young people in particular are not convinced that the answers to these questions which they have received at home, at school, or at church are relevant to their needs. And many thoughtful adults are themselves perplexed in their thinking about sex, love, marriage, and the home. They wish they knew how to think about the problems that seem to have overtaken all of us in this whole arena of life.

The fact is that most adults have themselves been the products of freer talk about sexuality but of nothing worth calling "sex education." Hence, as parents they have been faced with the task, even as they raised their families, of thinking out the part that sex should play in their own lives. Their experience may have taught them what to reject, but they are far from confident about the real basis for a positive philosophy of sex. They know that they do not want hush-hush attitudes or repressive silences about sex, nor do they want anything that smacks of hypocrisy.

Adults also sense as never before that the attitudes their children take to sex and love are part of larger, equally difficult questions. Yet they simply do not feel equipped to answer these questions. More aware than their own parents of the many factors involved in a full and free discussion of sex and love, they hardly feel prepared to offer the necessary guidance. Hence, they often ease their frustrations by adopting more "permissive" attitudes toward what their young people do, in the hope that a freer climate will at least prevent "negative" attitudes and psychological repression.

The author, himself a member of that generation of adults and parents, has had the privilege over the last twenty-five years—the days of his own parental experience with three sons—of discussing, largely with young people of high school and college age, questions relevant to their self-discovery. In about a hundred colleges, and in many more than a hundred young people's gatherings and conferences, he has talked, listened, and learned. What cannot be stressed enough is the desire of these young people for straightforward talk and a frank sharing of experience. What leaves an indelible impression is their increasing realization that sex, love, and marriage are somehow related to the other needs and dimensions of their lives.

In another day there also seemed to be general agreement, even among those who would have preferred to obey their first impulses and "do what comes naturally," that sex life does not exist in a vacuum. But today many are asking:

Now that we have miracle drugs and "foolproof" contraceptives, can we not partition sex off from the rest of life sufficiently to permit a freer and fuller sexual life while at the same time reducing the bad effects to a negligible minimum?

No intelligent person can disregard the possible far-reaching effects of recent scientific discoveries, involving drugs and contraceptives, on our thinking about sexual intercourse. Who would not expect informed young people, of college age especially, to raise questions about the validity of sex standards, once they are assured that sexual intercourse need not result in unwanted children? Furthermore, could alert young people remain unaffected when they hear their elders debating with new intensity the desirability of disseminating birth-control methods and of proper education in their use? After all, if married adults can and ought to use contraceptives to control birth, what good reason is there for condemning "safe" sexual intercourse for nonmarried persons?

On the surface, at least, and speaking in biological terms alone, there might seem to be no counterargument. But this book defends the claim that the *basic* argument against extramarital sexual intercourse is untouched by medical advances. Unfortunately, in high schools and on college campuses, as well as in the churches and homes of the land, there has been much more dismay at the presumed "moral revolution" than anything resembling education and thorough discussion. No amount of "information" about "what is going on" can provide systematic answers to the questions young people are raising. "Pills" they can buy; "precautions" they can take. But they are still wondering what place sex and love have in life and what they ought to bring to, and expect from, marriage.

The basic contention of this book is that these questions cannot be answered without thinking about related issues. We cannot know what the place of sex in the life of a person ought to be without asking: What values make for the growth of creative personality? This is a large question, and only a beginning can be made here. But nothing less can be called sex *education,* and no more far-reaching ques tion faces any person. The six chapters that follow are attempts to set sex, love, marriage, and home in relation to the total life of a person.

The home is the inner world in which human beings enter into their heritage as persons. We have become so preoccupied with new talk about sex that we have forgotten to ask what kind of homes, what patterns of value, persons need for their fulfillment as persons. Every marriage can create and destroy persons. It can make, or fail to make, a home for sex, love, and the person. In Chapter One this theme is opened up.

In Chapters Two and Three we focus on the questions usually neglected in the discussion of the place of sex and love: What kind of person is the goal of sex, love, marriage, and homemaking? How do we know the values that keep personality creative? Unless we have some conception of the pattern of values we ought to expect of ourselves, we cannot evaluate the goals we wish to realize through sex and love. At the same time, sex in particular cannot be treated in some preconceived way, and we need to reexamine some assumptions that govern our thinking about sex and love and their relation to marriage and the home. To this reexamination Chapters Four and Five are devoted.

The persistent question facing all of us is "Do sex and love need marriage?" Thoughtful people in every age have asked the question. But today the discovery of drugs and contraceptive devices force us to think our answer through again. And the answer will not be well-grounded, we suggest, unless we consider the conditions under which sex and love remain creative *for persons.* The question is not whether a person, single or married, can have sexual intercourse without anxiety and guilt. The question is "How can sex contribute to the strength and confidence that persons find when their lives have significance and design?"

In the first five chapters the intent is to present the main theme of this book with as little controversy as possible. But, as my discussions will show, there are underlying questions that keep on returning to challenge earlier conclusions. In Chapter Six we review earlier themes and attempt to become aware of the larger issues at stake as we determine our policy about the place of sex and love in our lives as persons. These underlying issues call for much more comprehensive discussion, to which the present effort hopefully may contribute.

The aim of this book, then, is to bring to bear upon our thinking about sex, love, and marriage a conception of the person and of the values that give meaning to his existence. Our aim is not to be polemic, but it may be suggestive here to indicate basic lines of agreement and divergence with some contemporary analyses.

For example, with Albert Ellis and Hugh Hefner there is agreement that our thinking toward sexuality should be free from arbitrary, negative attitudes that are oblivious to new knowledge about sex. But, we ask, how shall we define the goal of a person free to choose and free to fulfill himself? Without some conception of the kind of persons we can reasonably expect to be, we may overcome negativistic attitudes toward sex at the cost of creating deeper tensions. We may well encourage attitudes toward self and others that in fact keep sex from becoming a creative factor in the total value-growth of a person. I, for one, seem to detect in the "Playboy philosophy" a restricted vision of the person and a rather shallow appreciation of the dimensions of personal values; and I even wonder whether a new self-righteousness is not preening itself and parading in the name of modernity.

Again, a similar fear of restrictive codes and of self-righteous, insensitive moralism seems to me to lead thinkers like Joseph Fletcher and Bishop Robinson to conclusions that would not foster the very creativity they urge. In their attempt to avoid idolatry, to relate morality to personal growth at the expense of principles, do they really escape a relativity in morals that knows no direction? On what grounds can they defend love as the absolute, especially when they do not provide light as to its meaning (and cannot do so, I suggest, apart from some pattern of values)? In other words, it is not enough to say that freedom, or the love of persons, is the absolute value—especially if one does not provide also a criterion of value that will keep freedom from becoming emasculated power, and love from becoming self-absorption or sentimentality. What is at issue is not only the meaning of Christian love but the justification for any particular view of what it involves. As I try to show, in Chapters Two and Three especially, unless there is a supporting theory of values to guide us as we try to love both our enemy and our friend as persons, it will be easy to do almost anything in the name of love.

At the same time, it is not enough to propose as I do that there is an ideal pattern of values for all persons and that there are guiding principles and policies by which we do and can criticize our rules and codes. For the basic principle is that persons ought to respect and encourage the growth of values in themselves as persons in every situation. This is the minimum meaning of love, but it needs explication in terms of some such pattern of values as "the symphony of values" to be proposed.

Still, equally informed and sensitive persons can come to different conclusions about specific choices because they analyze differently the concrete cause and effect sequences among values in specific persons-in-community. Hence, I find myself taking a stronger stand against extra-marital intercourse than does the book *Sex and Morality* (the Report to the British Council of Churches). This careful statement, which came to hand only after the present manuscript was completed, is most helpful. But I would not be able to justify even the conclusions of this Committee without reference to a more explicit conception of the dynamics of value in personality. Nothing less is required, as we try to think both freshly and clearly about family planning, abortion, population control, and homosexuality, than sensitivity both to the scientific data at our disposal and to the interpenetration of values as human personality changes and grows. The present effort is the exploration of the interrelation of what seem to me to be reasonably well-established facts and values.

The occasion for bringing together ideas in most of this book was the invitation to deliver the Marmaduke H. Mendenhall Lectures at De Pauw University in February 1965. The friendly hospitality of Chaplain Elmer I. Carricker remains a warm memory. To the audiences there, and especially to President William E. Kerstetter, I am grateful for encouragement to work toward publishing the ideas I presented at De Pauw.

To my brother Angelo, I am once more indebted for co-authoring many thoughts that appear here. But a book of this sort cannot be written without a new sense of gratitude to my wife and three sons.

PETER A. BERTOCCI

Arlington, Massachusetts

CONTENTS

SEX, LOVE, AND THE PERSON

1 MARRIAGE: HOLY WEDLOCK OR UNHOLY DEADLOCK?

A Home or a Psychological Slum?

Whenever we are hard pressed to explain unwelcome changes in social attitude, we feel we can safely refer to "the breakdown of the home." For doesn't everyone agree that the home is the inescapable laboratory of human growth? No wonder, then, that the presumed changes in traditional sexual morals are also readily attributed to the breakdown of the home. But the home, that ancient source of life and habit, that refuge for feeling and memory, is a large and sprawling place. What ell or dormer is in need of attention? What part in particular has broken down?

My thesis is that what we call "the home" has never in reality succeeded in providing for certain critical factors in the formation of an adequate outlook on sex, love, and marriage. We have liked to think comfortably of the "home" as a basic social institution; we have counted on its "being there" without asking what it is and what it ought to be. We are inclined to wait too long before we ask: How shall we remodel our philosophy of home and keep it in constant repair if we and our children are to face new facts and values—including sex, love, and marriage—in their proper relation to each other?

"I have been married for ten years to a surgeon. I now hate him." These words—for I describe an actual situation —came from the lips of a woman, attractive, stylish, and of obvious good breeding. Reared in an upper middle-class family, graduated from a good college for women, she would seem by ordinary standards to have been endowed with the resources for happiness. But her story revealed that her house of life had been built on sand.

Let us imagine her parents at supper one evening reading a letter from their daughter in her junior year in college. " . . . Bill's just wonderful. And just think, he has asked me to marry him! I accepted, as you might have guessed. As soon as he finishes medical school, we want to be married." Mother and father look at each other with satisfied smiles that, among other things, mean: "Well, we did not send her to college in vain!"

Their daughter would have agreed. She had found her man; she would be no failure as a woman, in any case. Her fondest dream seemed about to be fulfilled. And Bill's parents liked her as much as her parents liked Bill.

The whole situation seemed so good, so normal. And we can rapidly fill in the incidents to come. The young people have a "nice" wedding surrounded by friends. With hard work and reasonable financial backing from their parents, they soon buy a house situated in an uncrowded suburb. In ten years, Bill becomes a well-respected surgeon in the area, a top man in his field. Their life would seem to promise the ideal success story: with no financial worries, a well-appointed one-family house in the "right" community, the "right" connections. Yet this stunned, grief-stricken woman hated her husband. Her marriage, holy wedlock, had become unholy deadlock. Why?

There is much more than meets the eye in such situations, and more than the unhappy woman knew. But let me summarize her words: "Bill is a successful surgeon; he has worked hard. But we have a seven-year-old son who is miserable and is under psychiatric care. He needs his father to be a father. And, I confess, beyond my desire for a sweetheart, I need the kind of partner Bill has never been. He thinks that once he has provided for us, the rest is up to me, and he blames me for our son's condition."

We cannot, of course, generalize from individual cases. I have merely sketched this one, however, because this marriage poignantly illustrates a number of generalizations that our common experience would confirm.

Bill's conception of what a home should be dominates many a man, whether factory worker or surgeon. His essential role is that of provider, and to his wife must fall the role of family-builder. If he can keep the family economically solvent and secure, he has done his job in marriage. He judges himself mainly by his relations to his male peers. His family life and the needs of his wife and his child, other than those created by biological, social, and economic pressures, enter his thinking only at the periphery of his existence. He cannot understand why things should go wrong. Has he not worked hard? Does he not have a right to relax without being bothered by home cares?

It would be easy to dismiss Bill as an extreme example. Yet at bottom, Bill's thinking illustrates an outlook which, because it seems so obvious, has been too readily condoned even by the church. Every marriage must have a solid economic basis, and every good husband must shine as a breadwinner! Actually, taken alone, it would be hard to find a more crassly materialistic conception of the basis for success in marriage.

What is really at issue—and what needs radical revision in the minds of most of us—is the meaning of "home." My definition places the emphasis upon other values that are also latent in much of our thinking. The home is an institution sanctioned by law, but rooted in the love that husband and wife feel for each other, and controlled by their commitment to the growth of each member of the family in the light of his needs and abilitites.

I believe this definition is valid and fruitful regardless of any assumptions about the existence of God. I have not said directly that the home is sanctioned by God or rooted in a particular faith in God. Yet I believe that we come to know God and His will in part as we discover that persons cannot grow unless their roots are nourished in responsive and responsible love. The home is the crucible that puts to the test two individuals committed to each other and to their family in discovering and sharing all the values in life open to them, including their faith in what is ultimate in the universe.

It is unlikely that this conception of a home lurked even vaguely in the background of Bill's thinking. At any rate, his wife, confronted with the maladjustments of their son, was forced to realize that something more than social status and economic security, something more than a house in the right section of town was needed to make a home for him as well as for herself. What was now incredible to her was that this truth had not been obvious from the beginning.

"Evidently," she said, "we did not really know each other very thoroughly, and we never made clear to ourselves what we thought made life worth living. I certainly gave little real thought to what kind of a father Bill would be or to what a home really required. And now I realize that the things we need most for our son are things that money cannot buy and that social position will not give."

Like so many others, this woman had been under the control of the idea that if one were "in love" with and married a decent chap who had a promising financial future, everything else could come of itself. Bill had fit the model that her own family life seemed to suggest and that dominated so much of the thinking around her. But she had now discovered for herself that such things as social position and economic security can become the masters of one's plans rather than servants. She and her husband postponed the birth of the baby until their one-family house was in sight; and after Billy came, they had kept putting off having another child. Bill's idea that in a home the father was exclusively the good provider and his wife's lack of confidence in her ability to cope with the whole business of having a number of children had brought on the situation. How could she raise a family and keep their social life going smoothly at the accustomed rate?

So here they were, one cold and rather bitter man, one discouraged and resentful wife, one child denied the benefits of a real companionship—all coexisting separately in a comfortable house.

The situation that the unhappy woman revealed to me was not unusual. She would not have been flattered to be told that she was not unusual in her mistakes. Bill, in particular, would have been amazed if informed that the house he had provided was a psychological slum-dwelling—not to say a spiritual orphanage for their son. A *psychological slum* is an atmosphere in which a human being finds it difficult to do much more than keep alive. In it there is little hope for his growth as a total person.

Bill's son knew him as a benefactor but not as a compan-

ion; Bill's wife, unable to cope with her own loneliness in
family matters, disappointed in her own capacity to be
what she felt somehow a mother should be to her son,
frustrated in her attempts to make a center of common
affections and values in the home, had become rather rigid
and censorious. Try as she might, she had failed to be the
steady source of emotional education and strength that the
son needed. She had found "her man" in college; she had
married the man of her dreams. But each now in fact
passed by the other under the same roof, because they were
estranged by disagreement about what matters most in life.
In this house the child had never found "living room."
Above all, he needed a chance to share his privileges with
other children, younger and older, both within and outside the family. But there were no bridges that he could
manage to build between himself and other children in
the school and neighborhood. This family lived under the
same roof, but there were impassable psychological distances; divorce had occurred although it had not yet become legal—in upper middle-class American style.

This marriage was very respectable; husband and wife
has been "faithful" to each other; they had given their
child the best that could be bought. It was the kind of
situation that seems to preserve all the accepted values and
yet casts doubt upon them. Consider the question: When
this man and woman, alienated in spite of their wordly
success, had sexual intercourse with each other, what was
the *quality* of their union? We may assume that their use
of adequate contraceptives removed fears of unwanted
pregnancies. We may assume that their understanding of
each other's emotional and physiological responsiveness
to sexual stimulation and caressing was such that harmonious orgasm could be theirs. I press the question: What

quality did such sexual union have in the lives of two persons who found themselves out of essential harmony in many other areas of their lives? I can report the wife's telling comment: "Sometimes I feel like a kept woman and not a partner in his life. I just cannot go on like this." And what countereffect had this attitude produced in her husband? Had he no feeling that his wife had become a stranger?

Obviously, my concern here is not to take sides. This marriage, even at the level of sexual value or meaning, was dying because two persons had entered into a compact with assumptions about life and about the making of a home that simply could not stand the test of intimate living. Their initial love had sought foundations in the promise of their financial stability and assured social status without inquiring about more basic values and compatibilities. The love with which they started their marriage simply could not take further root in their lives and develop new dimensions. They were not sufficiently aware of the other values needed to shape their lives and their marriage, to guide the proper nurture and education of a child, or, in a word, to create a home.

Love—Without Roots?

Without further comment I pass on to another interview, this one with a young lady in her senior year at a college for women. "I have been brought up a Protestant; my father is an active Episcopalian. I am very much in love with a Roman Catholic fellow. I am told," she said, "that our marriage could lead to serious problems, but I don't see why. Can you tell me?"

"Let's forget for the time being," I suggested, "the labels 'Protestant' and 'Catholic.' Does your sweetheart believe that in all matters of faith and morals the final authority is the Pope? Does he take his commitment to his life in the church seriously? For example, is he faithful in attendance at Mass and at Confession?" The answers were affirmative. "As far as you can see, does God mean something vital to his life, so that his daily living and thinking would be quite different without this faith?" Again, after a pause, the answer was yes. "In other words, you would say that God, as worshiped and served in and through the Roman Catholic Church, is fairly central to his life?" The answer was yes.

What I was after was a religious profile that went beyond family background and the conventional commitments and labels. In this instance, the profile came out clearly, its main lines reinforced by the remainder of our conversation. So I turned to her: "Do you believe that in all matters of faith and morals every man is a priest before God?" "What does that mean?" she asked. It soon became evident that her Protestantism was not even word-deep. "What does God mean to you?" I asked, and she replied, "I must confess that I have not thought seriously about God since the days when I used to look to Him to help me get across the street safely, when I was about six years old." "Does prayer have any place in your life?" "No." "What does the church mean to you?" "I go to please my parents, and especially my wonderful father. I know that if I marry a Roman Catholic, it will hurt him in a different way than it will hurt my mother. But he tells me this choice must be mine."

This young lady did not mind bringing up her children in the Catholic Church, provided that she did not herself join the church. We soon came to the basic contrast. Her fiancé and his values were inspired by the teachings of the church and his own experience of God. But her life was guided by the attitude "live and let live" (which amounted to little more than "let me alone to do what I want"). There was no common center of worship and meaning. She worshiped him but not his God. Her values were those of a decent, conventional person whose life and education had not succeeded in challenging her to think out her value-system. She admitted that she loved him, in part at least, because he seemed to propel his own ship. But they had "not really talked yet about religion."

Toward the end of our conference she remarked that she had never really appreciated how far they might be from each other at the level of religious consciousness, not to speak of religious knowledge and dedication. Her religious thinking had barely reached that of a critical adolescent. She was more vividly aware that, below the surface, her commitments in life were "spelled out in a different way" than her fiancé's. The drama of his existence was dominated by different actors. She had some sense that he conceived of his part in the drama of life quite differently than she did. "I could not share his prayer, his worship; and, I suppose, some of his basic joys and disappointments are just beyond me. I really don't live in his world. Perhaps I shouldn't marry him, not because he's a Catholic, but because I'm really nothing. My life has been a series of episodes, but his life seems to have a point."

It is important to understand persons below the level of their surface commitments and expressions, especially when values are in question. This interview had started with differences in church affiliation, but what emerged was the content or vitality of religious experience and belief in two lives, and the other values affected by these differences.

Any two persons, whether or not of the same faith, must seek to be as conscious as possible of what they are bringing to their marriage and to each other and their children. If these two young people shared any basic commitment to values, even excluding religion, they might still have started their marriage agreeing in their basic affirmations, those that married life itself can so quickly call into action. Without some common, vital pattern of values to guide lovers, every relationship in marriage will be weakened. A home becomes impossible. But when common meanings unite two lovers, even their sexual experience is influenced. I remember vividly the young married couple who said to me: "Our sexual experience means quite a lot to us; but sometimes we feel even closer when we pray to our God together. And when we decided consciously to share our faith in God by bringing a child into the world, our sex experience was out of this world."

Marriage—A Crucible for Love?

I add the experience of another couple as further evidence that the love of two persons is no stronger than their values, and that their marriage will be a crucible within which these values will be tested.

I had known Ann and Jim when they were undergraduates. Ann had been especially interested in child development and had taken a course in the philosophy of religion. Jim had concentrated in physics. Neither one was outwardly striking as a personality; both were rather shy and untalkative—I remember thinking that if they got married their first child would never learn to talk. Both were fairly conscientious, but again with no particular aim and very little sparkle. They got married, during World War II, and Jim went into the service. The baby came, unplanned, but they took him readily into the circle of their devotion. The war over, Jim went to graduate school, working for his Ph.D., as the saying goes, "by the sweat of his Frau"; Ann was typing his way through graduate school.

Then came that fateful Saturday morning. Jim had taken off early for his laboratory; Ann, hearing no voice from the crib and thinking that she might get that unusual extra little nap, rolled over and went sound asleep. The child was at that age when one did not know whether he could climb out of his crib. That morning he succeeded and crept out, exploring. Ten minutes later, Ann found him dead on the bathroom floor; he had swallowed a disinfectant.

It was two years after this that Ann wrote to me. "I knew that you were somewhat concerned about my marriage to my quiet man, that you thought I wasn't ready for marriage, and I confess that the war tended to hurry things a bit. I remember your saying once that the most fundamental transition in life was from 'I want to be loved' to 'I want to love,' and that any marriage would soon feel the effects of one's development in this respect. When our baby came into our lives, our love for each other took on a new form. Jim loved me, but I felt he loved me in a richer, more grateful way as little Ted grew, and in Ted our lives seemed to take a direction and shape that somehow made the agony of the war years more worth-while.

"When I saw our baby dead on the bathroom floor, everything I had built, all the meanings of my life, and above all my partnership with Jim, fell into ashes around me. For the last two years my life has been a hell, and I can't tell you what it must have meant for Jim to live with me. Every bit of confidence I ever had—and you know I didn't have too much—every bit of our working together during the war and in the graduate-school years disappeared; and Jim had to go on, to live with his own grief, and, in spite of my condition, complete his work.

"How many times I have re-read my notes and tried to rethink those discussions on the problem of evil—and I'm glad I know that our problem was one that greater minds than mine have grappled with. But as I look back at the last two years now, I think I know what has brought me back to wanting to live again, as opposed to forcing myself to stay alive.

"When they called Jim home from the laboratory that Saturday, I shall never forget what happened when he got there. I was beside myself with grief, of course, and knowing how much he cared for Ted, I did not know what was going to happen. But he came into the room, and even with Ted right there in the next room, came over to me and took me into his arms, crying, 'Ann, I love *you*,' over and over again.

"That quiet man of mine had certainly made the transition you had talked about. How much it has been tested in the past two years! His own anguish at the loss of Ted was deeper than he could express—but here I was in a shambles. Do you remember how you used to talk about quarantining evil, that if we couldn't prevent it we could at least keep it from spreading? Well, this man of mine has devoted himself to his work and to me with unremitting effort; bit by bit he has been putting me together again, and this letter to you is to say that I think I am on the mend. Jim's love for me has been able to break down the walls I have put up against him.

"As my teacher, perhaps you'll pardon me for being so frank—but my experience called up again one of the questions I've heard you suggest. 'What must it be like for a husband to have sexual intercourse with a wife who feels that she is not worthy of him, who nevertheless "complies" with his need and, occasionally, with her own aroused passion?' Why Jim did not give me up, I'll never know; he certainly did not stay with me because of what I could bring even to our sexual embrace. He *loved* me—and the clause 'in sickness and in health' doesn't begin to express what he has been through! He loved *me* for myself, and I was more to him than the unsolved problem he was collecting data about in his laboratory. I was part of his life, and he has sewn me together by the cords of his love. Oh, how married we are now! Nobody could give herself more completely to him, and our marriage has grown new roots. Yes, I feel our baby moving in me now, and I have hope. Ted will always be a part of our lives, but in dying he has gradually brought new meaning into our love. But what a price we paid for this new meaning, this new love, this new hope!

"Yes, I have heard a lot in my church about sin being wiped clean by love, about repentance and redemption. I say to you that I know what this means in my life; I have lived it beyond the preaching. The man who loved me and would not let me go even when I had let our tragedy—I used to call it my sin—separate us, the man who held my hand when I had my relapses of despair, the man who made me part of the work and meaning of his life when his work too might have become meaningless—that man has taught me what redeeming love can be! The God I had *talked* about but never felt—that God came alive to me anew in and through Jim, my lover, my husband, my partner. I just want you to know."

The experience of Ann and Jim, set beside that of the surgeon and his wife, can throw a dramatic light upon some of the issues we need to face.

A marriage, clearly, is not an appendage to love that justifies sex and makes two persons legally responsible to each other and their progeny. A marriage is a crucible into which two persons let themselves be thrown. Daily interaction, at every level of their personalities and being, will test all that they have been. It will put their love to work, creating and re-creating. It will take for granted that human existence is a challenge. From the first, it will involve emotional commitments and attitudes surprisingly resistant to change, sometimes supporting, sometimes repulsing each other, pulling together and pushing apart lives that hoped to find in marriage unity and strength.

Is Marriage Only a Social Convention?

I have often heard it said that marriage is something society forces upon young people. To be sure, this comment often comes from young lovers who wish to know why they should refrain from sexual intercourse until marriage. For them there is something artificial about controlling their desire for union with each other "until we are married in a church before a lot of people, few of whom we know well." My full comment on this view of marriage will emerge later, but some considerations may be advanced now.

To young people who feel not only the normal, strong

demands of their sexual emotions but also a deeper demand of their love to close every distance between them, it will always seem extrinsic and artificial to wait for marriage. But their objections to waiting will be all the more likely if they think of marriage as only a social convention, or even as merely instrumental to their love for each other. And for two persons "in love" it seems ridiculous to suppose that their love, whose strength seems so overpowering, may not be the lasting foundation for their marriage, especially if they can keep the wolf from the door.

I suggest that they cannot know the full meaning of either their sexuality or their love without marriage and a home. Theirs is a situation analogous to that of the poet who must find a form through which to discover what he really means and to make it enduring. Sex means more when it expresses love. Both sex and love will grow in meaning only as they are invested in and dedicated to a home that expresses and externalizes the values that give meaning to their existence. When they say: "We are married when we love each other," they are correct, in a sense. So can the poet say that the sense of inspiration makes him a poet; yet, in one way or another, poets have always called on the Muses for witness and for aid.

I ask such young people, impatient and not fully aware of the meaning and difficulty of their enterprise: Do you really mean that a formal vow to each other in the presence of all you hold dear and also to representatives of a society in which you must live can add no further depth and purpose to your love? I doubt that the answer can be negative, but I need to lay firmer grounds for my position.

I would agree that if two persons do love each *other,* they are indeed married in spirit, and no marriage *is* a marriage that is not a marriage of the spirit. Yet that very spirit involves the overwhelming concern that they join their lives together not simply in the sexual experience but in that common sharing that only actual marriage and dedication to a home make possible. Spirit, to make itself manifest and to survive, must embody itself in the acts that it informs. If the love of these two young people does mean that they want to draw near to each other, for better or worse, in a common responsibility, and in sickness and in health, marriage alone will allow them to share their quest for values fully. And if this is so, why not celebrate this purpose symbolically in the presence of others who have given themselves to this couple's good—their families and their friends? Why not enforce their purpose with all the imaginative support of ritual?

For the marriage ceremony is love becoming mature enough to take a public stand, gladly and solemnly, before all that is holy in life. It is to perform the movements of ritual in public, to say out loud what the young couple began to say when they started to "go together," when they expressed their affection and promised their loyalty to each other by the gesture of gifts and then by an engagement ring. The marriage ceremony is not the end of the inner dance they felt when they fell in love; but it is to make it known by taking formal steps, showing before all men that they wish to accept responsibility for everything that they can possibly possess and share. The marriage vow is love that takes itself deeply and seriously enough, that has become reflective enough and firm enough to be willing to risk a public promise to resist the urgings of self-love, to abjure parasitism, and to create an enduring center for the human enterprise. The husband may change or increase the radius and depth of his work—what he will not alter is his pledge to be loyal to his wife and to share storm and sunshine with her. The home will be the crucible in which they with their children will work out some of the central meanings of their existence. It is this dedication without reservation to a shared quest for value and significance that will make a family into a home.

Marriage and home, then, are intrinsic to the growth of meaning in love; in this atmosphere persons provide for each other. Marriage gives love and sex the opportunity to sift a workable ideal from a mere dream and to discover a stable pattern of life. To go from breakfast dishes through daily work to bed is a crucial test, and it introduces into experience many unsuspected possibilities of failure and success. To have been married even five years is enough for any couple to know that they now love each other for a whole range of reasons quite different from those they would have given before their marriage. In other words, marriage can indeed be a threat to sex and love, but the threats would have been there without marriage, and they would have had to be faced by individuals unfortified by a social declaration of their commitment. Every reason that makes lovers "quake" before marriage is a reason for getting married and beginning the work of building their home.

From a Marriage to a Home

Love, I have been urging, needs marriage if it is to grow. It can die in marriage, but, as I shall argue later, it is more likely to die without marriage. In any case, further argument is hardly needed for asserting that the home cannot just happen; it does not simply follow after marriage. Out-

ward circumstances do not guarantee a home any more
than does a love barren of values and ideals. Yet at every
stage in history it is important to take into account changes
in circumstances that can challenge, threaten, and promote
the values marriage and home create. It seems to me that
the most important changes in our day are encouraging
us to be persons and not males and females. They are
changes that also force us to take a closer look at what
justifies the demand for a home of the sort I am defin-
ing.

Many industrial and social changes have made it possible for women to earn their own living and to feel less
dependent upon men for financial security. Their schooling is not inferior to that of men, and they now can take
their places side by side with men in store, office, factory,
and in political life. They often demand more of themselves and of men in the total life of a community. Their
challenge to rigid ideas about "man's work" and "woman's
work" can produce better conditions for all, provided
more mature patterns of expectation and conduct can be
developed. Thus they can ask for more help from their
husbands in the making of a home; the family can be a
primary concern for both husband and wife as they think
of their future together.

But there will be chaos if the "new freedom" for women
produces only defensive counterattitudes in men and
merely releases women from the evils of overdependence—
without increasing their status as persons or their responsibility in the task of building a home. What is needed is a
reappraisal of men's attitudes toward women that will ac-
cord with the higher conception of women as persons and
not merely as females, a reappraisal that will lead to a
rethinking of the demands that a real home makes upon
men and women.

In particular, the new freedom given men and women to plan the birth of children needs to be carefully evaluated. What is it that makes sex a creative or destructive factor in the lives of human beings? The development of contraceptive aids has undermined the basis of the double standard which encouraged laxity in men while imposing sexual restraint upon women. The new ease of birth control through contraceptives may have its dangers, but it also forces us to a deeper and truer virtue in matters of sex. From now on, a sexual morality must be based upon a clearer view of the conditions that protect and enhance the *values* sex can bring to human experience and to the home.

For it is quite clear that the significant and sometimes justifiable extrinstic factors that encouraged persons to make a career of marriage need not operate any longer. If a "home" was based largely on these extrinsic factors, rooted as they are in economic, social, and biological status, such a home now rests on shifting sands. If a "home" resulted from the necessity of protecting the children that sexual experience would bring, appropriate contraceptives may now be counted on to remove that necessity. But if a home is an institution built on the free aspiration of two persons and their vow to be responsible for each other's total creative welfare, then its foundations are as solid as thoughtful human motivation can make them. Such a home will be based squarely on real human needs.

To be human is to need other human beings—for safety, for health, and for fulfillment of one's uniquely human needs and abilities. No human being is self-made—because he cannot possibly survive and grow in isolation from other persons who accept responsibility for protecting him in weakness and supporting him in strength. But no human being can treat other human beings as if they were things without destroying the finest possibilities of human nature both in himself and in others. This means that he needs to be understood by others, that he needs others to help him discover his potential in the midst of his uncertainties, especially from infancy to late adolescence. One psychologist has reminded us that human growth normally moves from dependence to independence to dependability.

We hardly needed modern psychology to tell us that the kind of parents a child has and the attitude they take toward him, both in his dependence and independence, will have much influence on the degree and kind of dependability he will develop. Modern psychology has made us better able to diagnose and take into account the pitfalls and opportunities in human development, especially as these are affected by the family environment. Apart from any of the adult needs that husband and wife help each other to satisfy, parents are surely needed by both child and adolescent. But the way in which they need each other, and are needed by child and adolescent, goes far beyond survival and comfort. They need support for each other's total growth as persons. This is a matter of values. For the moment, let us say that these values are shrewd guesses as to what parents and children must have, collectively and individually, if they are to attain a quality of life that is truly human.

A home, consequently, is a moral structure made from a quest on the part of two or more people for values that can be achieved together and shared with children as they enter into a larger society as independent beings. The home provides the conditions in which all members of the family make the effort required to bring to fruition their potential as persons, as far as this lies within the powers of the family. A family starts with the husband's and wife's commitments to values. These values are tested and modified, particularly when children begin to play their part in determining what the family can become.

Essential to a home, then, is a willingness to share in the quest for values open to each member. Persons who marry, as we have seen, bring together their own personalities with all of their strengths and weaknesses. They will live in the same space, but they can walk past each other without seeing; they can collide with each other in their blindness both to their own value-possibilities and to those of their children and of others beyond the family. Or perhaps they will find harmonies they little realized existed before marriage, when they walked alone. Their "space" may now become a fortifying spirit of mutual concern and confidence that the greatest trials of life can shake but never destroy.

Human life is subject to thrusts that can bring out weakness and strength. All kinds of mishaps beyond either person's control can overtake them. Therefore, the overriding consideration becomes the vow two persons take in the presence of their parents, their friends, their society, their God. Their vow is to fuse their quests for value in such a way that they will not allow even their disagreements and weaknesses to separate them from their central goal of cherishing each other. There would be no point in taking a vow unless two persons did realize that, in their living together, psychological or spiritual distances could arise; their vow is that whatever these distances might be, each will do everything in his power—with the help of God, where God is a factor in their lives—to minimize the evil and maximize the good.

To put the matter differently, in the personalities of almost any married couple some factors in their commit-

ment to values will make for partial divisions or "divorce."
Actually, these are not so different from those they experienced when they were unmarried—even with their best
friends and within their families. What the marriage vow
means is that the two people are sufficiently confident
about the good things, about the values that do bind them
together, that they can overcome their differences. They
believe that the values they have in common will stand by
them when they face adversity and that they can come
even closer to each other as they join their lives together.
Adversity will come, married or unmarried. Let it now
come, with this person as one's partner; and let adversity
not come to one without the other there to bear it also.
Indeed, this partner can hurt as no one else can, can disap-
point to the point of despair; but this partner can also give
hope in the midst of defeat, can give new life when one
"wants to die."

In this chapter, I have been discussing sex, love, marriage, and the overarching need for a home to promote and
protect the growth of persons. At every point the discussion has come back to basic needs, commitments, and
values. The difference between a house and a home is one
of values. The difference between passion and love is one
of values. Indeed, what makes a person is his values; to
speak of a person's growth is to speak of his growth in
terms of values.

What values? How shall we think about values? It is to
this question that the discussion now takes us. I purposely
do not move directly to some of the major questions about
sex and love because, as I shall try to show, we cannot
make intelligent decisions without asking what the values
are that keep us growing as persons.

2 WHAT GIVES EXPERIENCES THEIR VALUE?

Maxims Are Not Enough!

"Be mature!" "Be integrated!" "Be well-rounded!" "Develop a wholesome and balanced personality!" Such maxims as these have been guiding much thinking about the goal of personality growth. The imperative: "Be democratic!" might have been added to this list, along with many others. And yet, if a parent asks: "What does it *mean* to be well-balanced? What goes into the making of a 'democratic' or mature personality?" does any pattern of personality take shape before our minds?

I do not object to any of these maxims as such. Nor do I object to such imperatives as: "Be a Christian!" "Follow Jesus!" "Love your neighbor!" "Do unto others as you would have them do unto you!" "Put God first!" But like the maxims already mentioned, they give little guidance until we begin to translate them into much more concrete ways of thinking and acting. Then we should probably disagree about what they meant. For instance, does "Be Christian!" as a general statement mean anything more than "Be well-balanced!"? Some think the two slogans are equivalent; others are sure they are not.

Everything, then, seems to depend on how we use these terms. That is why, if we are to avoid confusion and the weakness and waste it entails, we must carry our analysis deeper until we hit bedrock. The conviction that has been growing in me through the years—as a philosopher, as a parent, as a teacher, as an American citizen, as a professing Christian—is that we need desperately to set before us some pattern of values, some ideal of personality that will turn our vague maxims into operative goals. Only then will it be possible for a parent who wants his child to become mature or "to grow up a Christian" to have some directive idea of what feelings, habits, and traits of personality he wants to encourage and discourage in his children.

Let me illustrate by taking a philosophical slogan—the famous Kantian maxim: Respect persons, yourself and others, as ends in themselves and never as means only. This means in part: "Don't treat persons like things that cannot think and understand. Remember that persons can reflect on their lives and make up their own minds about what is good for them." Yet even this interpretation is not as helpful as it may sound unless I know what persons are, can be, and ought to be. How can I be justified in expecting certain powers of thought and understanding, a certain capacity for moral action in the persons with whom I deal, unless I have some tenable conception of what they can be at their best? Do I not need to keep in mind some model of man in order to know how to behave with full respect toward my neighbor?

I can already hear the chorus of objectors. "We hope you aren't thinking of drawing up some nice little diagram of what a person ought to be. Surely you know that people are so different and our knowledge so skimpy that it would be most hazardous—if at all possible—to construct a model by which we can guide human growth. We have had enough experience with lists of virtues, scales of values, and we want no Procrustean beds, even in the name of high morality. The result of your effort will be another moralism, a set of rules or standards so abstract that they will fail to apply to any real man anywhere at any time. Unable to follow them, men may either pretend to do so and become hypocrites, or they may develop a morbid sense of guilt at their failures."

Certainly these objections should serve as warning. But what is our alternative? Over-all models of human potentiality may have their dangers, but we wonder whether maxims were not distilled in the first place from actual ways in which human beings—some greater than others—lived. As long as they remain empty of content we easily find ourselves falling into the rigidity of customs and the stereotypes favored by some uncriticized way of life or by society's traditions. We do not in fact escape a model of personality; we merely become the servants, even the slaves, of an implicit model that we follow unawares.

Did not Jesus, for all His emphasis upon the spirit, suggest certain ways in which the spirit of love for God and neighbor become manifest without, of course, describing the specific act? Thus, for example, He enjoins:

"Blessed are the poor in spirit: for theirs is the kingdom of heaven.

"Blessed are they that mourn: for they shall be comforted.

"Blessed are the meek: for they shall inherit the earth.

"Blessed are they that hunger and thirst after righteousness: for they shall be filled.

"Blessed are the merciful: for they shall obtain mercy.

"Blessed are the pure in heart: for they shall see God.

"Blessed are the peacemakers: for they shall be called the sons of God.

"Blessed are they that have been persecuted for righteousness' sake: for theirs is the kingdom of heaven.

"Blessed are ye, when men shall reproach you, and persecute you, and shall say all manner of evil against you falsely, for my sake" (Matt. 5:3–11 A.S.R.*).

And did not St. Paul translate the meaning of love into virtues that would keep love from becoming a sounding brass or a tinkling cymbal?

"Love is patient and kind; love is not jealous or boastful; it is not arrogant or rude.

"Love does not insist upon its own way; it is not irritable or resentful; it does not rejoice at wrong, but rejoices in the right.

"Love bears all things, believes all things, hopes all things, endures all things.

"Love never ends; as for prophecies, they will pass away; as for tongues, they will cease; as for knowledge, it will pass away" (I Cor. 13:4–8 R.S.V.**).

Much as Jesus and Paul realized that man was not made for any precept, that no law could ever be allowed to trap man's potential before God, they realized that maxims, valuable as they are, need to be further related to the concrete situations in which men must make their choices. When there is no guiding pattern for growth, a personality easily becomes a patchwork of makeshift adjustments.

* American Standard Revision.
** Revised Standard Version.

We can escape moralism and idolatry, I believe, and at the same time discover a pattern of values in the light of which our own growth and the development of our children can be directed. Certainly, we shall never be able to make intelligent choices about sex, love, and marriage until we see what they mean in relation to the kind of human beings we prefer to be. In briefest outline, then, let us consider one possible way in which we seem to proceed when we make choices and see whether a pattern of values —what I like to call a symphony of values—begins to take shape in the personality.[1]

Discovering Values in Personal Experience

Let us assume that John is born to a couple who cares about his growth as a person. He has come into their lives not as a threat to their love for each other but as an expression of their love and commitment to each other; to their sense of security and intimacy, he adds a new dimension in love. They are anxious to know what he is like in himself; they want to be careful not to press his nature into some preconceived mold or ideal. He is to be neither an idol nor a slave; they, as parents, hope to avoid being tyrants.

Is there any principle they may follow that is basic to all human growth and creativity? I believe there is: *Act and plan with as clear an understanding as possible of what a person's needs and abilities are in any given immediate situation and in the foreseeable future.* To "understand"

---

[1] Elsewhere, such a pattern has been suggested—a symphony of values that will not override individuality and that will foster creativity. Peter A. Bertocci and Richard M. Millard, *Personality and the Good: Psychological and Ethical Perspectives* (New York: McKay, 1963), Chapters 14–17.

John does not necessarily mean to let John have whatever he says he wants, and thereby to neglect consideration of John's present and future responsibilities. But it does require an effort to know John as he is and for his own sake, before we lay out ideals for him and assess his responsibilities.

John's parents cannot even begin to care for him without acting on a broad principle or policy that has itself not been proved: Treat children as far as possible as ends in themselves and never as means only. These parents might never express this idea, in so many words, as a principle; they might never even have heard of Immanuel Kant. But Kant, as already suggested, was expressing the truth that we cannot relate ourselves to persons effectively unless we understand as far as possible what they are like in and for themselves, as well as in their possible relation to others. John from infancy onward must be understood as a person who can feel, will, and think, who can become involved increasingly in the plans that concern him and others.

"Parental love" can mean many things. But can it ever mean more than self-love unless it involves respect for the needs and abilities of the growing person in every situation and relationship? Must a loving person not assume that another human being's abilities and needs are as important as his own until evidence is advanced to prove the contrary? There is nothing "sentimental" about love expressive of this principle, as we shall see; it calls for the utmost honesty with all the facts about ourselves and others, good and bad, welcome and unwelcome, in every situation as a basis for policy. It requires all the insight and knowledge available in working out ideals.

From Experiencing to Evaluating

Let us, then, trace two main steps in the process of evaluation. First, as persons we find ourselves enjoying some experiences and hence desiring them to continue; we find other experiences unenjoyable and do not want them to continue. The wanted or desired experiences issue in what we may call *value-claims,* the undesired in *disvalue-claims.* If persons had no wanted experiences at all, there would be no value-experiences; no persons, no values, for values are experiences as felt and wanted, or as felt and unwanted (disvalue). Because each value-experience may issue in an uncritical claim that it is better than another, we may name this first uncriticized moment of actual value- or disvalue-experience "value-claim" and "disvalue-claim." The problem is to evaluate our value- and disvalue-claims.

For all that glitters is not as golden as it seems. Further, we want experiences that conflict with each other; we want tasty, calorific meals, but we also want to avoid obesity. As T. S. Eliot puts it in *The Cocktail Party,* "at the moment you were offered something you wanted, you wanted something else."[2] We are, therefore, forced to take a second and more reflective step and evaluate these spontaneous value-claims. We wish to know which of them are intrinsically most gratifying and also stand in supportive relation to other value-claims.

To take a very simple example: John enjoys the taste of sweets more than the food mother serves as his first course. Preferring this intrinsic, wanted value-experience to the other, he claims that it is better than the other (after all, he knows nothing about their body-building properties).

[2] T. S. Eliot, *The Cocktail Party* (New York: Harcourt, Brace & World, Inc., 1950).

His mother does and she will give him "sweets" only if he finishes all the food on his plate. He may nevertheless decide to accept these unwanted "finishing the food" disvalues as *instrumental* to the goal of experiencing the intrinsic value of tasting sweets. Gradually he himself discovers what his elders have already discovered, that if he eats too many sweets immediately before his meal or if in general he eats too many sweets, this enjoyment interferes with other enjoyments. At another time in his life he may be told by his dentist and doctor that he must forego certain sweets entirely, for while they taste good, their effect on him will keep him from enjoying other experiences of value he actually prefers. Better your own teeth than the best dental plates, better good health than diabetes or heart strain from overweight! Sometimes he will find himself substituting what did not taste good to begin with (a disvalue-claim) for what he had once enjoyed (a value-claim): coffee straight may be preferred to coffee with cream and sugar, once one gets used to it!

In *evaluating* his value-claims and disvalue-claims, we note, John, with the help of others, must think out the connection of each value-claim in the light of other value-claims. He must know certain facts about himself now and as he may become. He needs to go beyond the surface-glitter to value-experiences that are not only immediately desired but also dependably desired because they support more of the other value-claims he wants for himself and in relation to others.

Let us see how these two first steps, experiencing and evaluating value-claims, apply to sex, for example. John, say at the age of 4, may find quite accidentally that manipulating his penis is pleasant (value-claim); the experience of manipulating is pleasant in its own way (value-claim), just as the experience of urinating is pleasant, especially after he has postponed it until he could get to a toilet. Both experiences are value-claims; they both have their own quality of gratification.

What happens when John undergoes toilet-training? We may imagine that John has found greater enjoyment in his mother's approval (value-claim) of his inhibiting his urination (disvalue-claim) until he could find the toilet. Earlier in his life he had found that simply releasing his urine whenever he wanted to was pleasant (value-claim), but as he grew older he found unpleasant consequences (or disvalue-claims), that is, ungratifying experiences in wetting himself and in his mother's disapproval or his older brother's taunts. The ungratifying disvalue-experiences, in balance, encouraged him to postpone the intrinsically gratifying value-experience of urinating. For now he could avoid the discomfort of being wet (disvalue-claim), enjoy his mother's approval (value-claim), forestall his brother's taunts (value-claim), and have a feeling of "I can do it" about meeting expectations (value-claim). In other words, as John related value-claims to disvalue-claims, his evaluation led him to forego one gratifying, wanted experience for the sake of others.

John may find his experience of masturbating[3] much harder to evaluate. Using our labels "value-claim" and "disvalue-claim," let us consider a possible route of evaluation. Suppose now that his mother, finding him having the intrinsically gratifying experience of manipulating his

[3] The discussion here on masturbation is not intended to lead to a specific conclusion regarding masturbating, although it is intended to suggest the importance of the child's knowing, as he grows, what the consequences can be, and why he should or should not masturbate, in light of other values at stake (such as his own feeling of self-esteem). See p. 99 below.

penis, slaps his hand, scolds him, and in other ways mani-
fests her disapproval, saying that he must "never" do this.
Assume also that she neither now, nor even later, explains
why he should not do this, or that she even hints at awful
things that might happen to him. There is nothing in his
own experience that shows him unwanted or bad effects.
Without being told, or without understanding why he
should not masturbate, he may well find himself enjoying
an experience about which he nevertheless feels anxiety
because of the unwanted disapproval of his mother. "I'm
not hurting myself. I'm not hurting her. And I'm feeling
good until I find myself wondering what awful thing
might happen to me—and, anyway, I want mom to approve."

Obviously, this 4-year-old may not go through this explicit process of evaluating. It is no easy matter for a parent who might not mind John's masturbating much later
to know how to get across to her 4-year-old son that a value-
experience *now* can lead to ungratifying consequences that
he can't imagine later. But the parent must decide how in
this instance to express disapproval without having her
youngster come to associate unnecessary and undesirable
anxiety with a whole area of his body and his life.

In any case, these examples are simple instances of a
continuing process in John's life and in his parents': sifting
value-claims, or evaluating them by relating them to other
value-claims in one's own life and in others'. These two
main steps in the evaluation of value-experience, and our
illustrations, bring four further facts about ourselves and
our value-experiences into focus.

First, some experiences are probably never values or
valuable in themselves; they become valuable because they
lead to other experiences that by themselves are always

enjoyed. The experiences of the dentist's drill or a surgical operation, or refraining from immediate masturbation-pleasure become valuable because they help to ensure other value-experiences that we prize for their own sakes. This means that in further evaluating any value-claim, regardless of its primary quality in immediate experience, we always ask whether it stands in supportive or threatening relation to other intrinsic values.

Second, some value-claims may turn out to be very reliable and dependable, and for them we reserve the word *authentic* because *they are intrinsically valued and do cohere with other values.* Both of these conditions must be fulfilled, for we cannot condemn or affirm even intrinsic values as better or worse than each other unless we see to what degree they support each other. To look forward in our discussion, John will find that a kiss or a caress is an intrinsically valuable experience, but that it will mean more to him if it can be the expression of appreciation and love without endangering other wanted experiences in his life. The wanted and approved always interact with the unwanted and unapproved in his own life, just because he is the sort of person he is. He cannot assume that experiences are not affected by other experiences, that what tastes good will always taste good or will protect other values he wants; he must be wary about "forever blacks" and "forever whites" in his experiences. Why? Because he changes and because the contexts of his values change as he moves from situation to situation.

In short, we must keep in mind that in our human experience, where change—be it growth or decay—is always taking place, we must always evaluate any initial value-experience and value-claim by its relationships to the larger context of value-experiences we believe to be open to man. When I use the term *value* hereafter, I shall mean value-claims that have been found on the whole to be authentic or reliable within the context of human life as a whole.

A third realization grows out of the first two. Every evaluation is made on the basis of something that takes place in human beings, in their varied ways of development, and in their relations to one another in this world. *Values and disvalues are facts about what the persons who hold them are and can become in a world that both nurtures and challenges, encourages and destroys. Any value, in turn, is a fact about what the world can become in relation to the persons experiencing it.* The surgeon (in Chapter 1, p. 4) who thought that he could be only a biological father and a good breadwinner found that he could not keep the appreciation of a wife and nurture a 7-year-old son who needed him in other ways. There were facts about his life, about their lives, that he failed to see, and they destroyed the possibility of a home for himself and for them.

Fourth, we must not miss the distinction between *value-experience* and *value-possibilities,* or *value-potentials.* A potentiality, or possibility, for value or disvalue is not itself a value or disvalue. Value and disvalue are actual human experiences, realized or in process of being realized. A boy has the value-potentiality for fatherhood, but the value of his being a father cannot be experienced or assessed until he has actualized, or realized, the potential. Analogously, the value-possibilities of certain airwaves for the human experience of radio do not become values until persons discover them and experience radio programs.

In sum, we can now emphasize that there are no values without persons and their potentials for value-experiences.

At the same time, the values persons realize depend not only on their desiring but upon the total structure of the world in which persons live and realize themselves. A vein of gold in an uninhabited and unknown island has no value, but once discovered by people it is valuable only because it can be related to a gold standard set up by human beings. We cannot know what human beings really are until we know the range of their value-experiences, and we cannot know that value-experiences are reliable until we learn what value-potentialities and value-possibilities exist in them and in their world. Thus neither John nor his parents can evaluate the immediate gratifying value-experiences of masturbating or of kissing until they know which value-possibilities are encouraged and which are discouraged in his own life and in that of those affected by his experiencing. Human beings are always in process—not necessarily in progress—and all they have as a guide is their own experience of themselves and of the world in which they live.

On Knowing God's Will

If we are to discover a pattern of values that can be a reliable model for personality growth, we must keep our evaluations close to actual and possible human experience of value and trace the web and texture of interrelation among values. We cannot arbitrarily turn away suggestions of value because they are strange to us. Our prophets have been condemned because they have said to us in effect: "Your present way of life is endangering other possibilities open to you and to others. Turn, therefore, from the evil of your ways, and even from many of your present goods,

and make the next march forward in value-experience."
The story of Abraham being commanded to set forth from
Ur of the Chaldees, the story of Jesus and the rich young
ruler are dramatic illustrations. Implicit in such com-
mands is the conclusion: "For only by taking the next step
can you know what further riches are possible in the world
God has given you, in the potential with which he has
endowed you in your relationships with others in this
world."

"But is this the way to learn the will of God for man?"
some will ask. Only a limited answer is possible here, and it
draws out the implications of what has been said. We do
not know God's will in its full meaning and detail once
and for all. A revelation or rule illuminates a direction
and provides a moral and religious impetus; it does not
furnish a static blueprint. Love thy neighbor! What an
inspiring challenge! Yet it still requires actual experience
on man's part with his fellow men in this world to know
what love means and how it shall be implemented. Our
human problem is always to work out the meaning of
God's will concretely in our lives. This we can discover
only by seeing what happens to our natures when we follow one line of feeling, thought, and action rather than
another.

Perhaps I can illustrate my meaning by commenting on
a passage that, though found in Micah, gives graphic expression to the message of Hosea also. In Micah 6:8 A.S.R.
we read: "He hath showed thee, O man, what is good; and
what doth Jehovah require of thee, but to do justly, and to
love kindness, and to walk humbly with thy God." (In the
Revised Standard Version, the meaning given to "kindness" is "steadfast love.") In Hosea 12:6 A.S.R. we read:
"Therefore turn thou to thy God: keep kindness and jus-

tice, and wait for thy God continually." But how do we know the relationship between "steadfast love" and "justice"? They often seem to conflict with each other drastically. How do we decide whether to be kind or to be just? Indeed, why not say, "Do kindness and love justice"?

I am aware that I am wandering into an area where experts disagree,[4] and without any pretense that what I am about to say could be adequately justified by the text, let me take liberties that will help me to illustrate more concretely how we might decide why it is a better interpretation of the will of God to say "do justice and love mercy."

Hosea, let us assume, is speaking to his people about their unfaithfulness to the God who has led them out of Egypt and who has kept His promises in the covenant that Israel then made with Him. Should God continue to be faithful or should He allow an outraged "justice" to take its course? How does Hosea know what God will do? It would be easy to close the question by saying that Hosea's answer was revealed as God's will and leave it there, whether we understand the command or not. But until we see how mercy and justice are related in the texture of our lives—the human texture that we do not create all by ourselves—our choice is likely to be impulsive rather than wise.

I sometimes think that we misread the Bible by misinterpreting the meaning of the dramatic form in which it is presented. Thus God is represented as telling Abraham, already a man past his prime, to tear up roots and venture with his family into an unknown country. Are we to think of a situation in which Abraham is sure of the presence of Jehovah in the same sense as he is sure of the walls of his

[4] See James M. Ward, *Hosea: A Theological Commentary* (New York: Harper and Row, 1966).

tents? Wherein, then, would his "faith" consist? If Abraham's "faith" is to be thought real, must not the coming of God to him be considered the illumination of ways of thinking, feeling, imagining, and acting in Abraham that prepared him for the call of God? In the case of Moses, is it nothing that God should use, to deliver His people out of Egypt, a Hebrew who had already shown that, far from identifying himself with the princely class of Egyptians by whom he had been luckily adopted, he had found it in his heart to sympathize with his oppressed brothers by blood?

The situation of Hosea is similar. The "steadfast love" that Jehovah offers His people instead of the rigors of justice could be realized as an alternative only by a person who, betrayed in a most intimate relation of life, nevertheless finds it in his heart to forgive his unfaithful wife. It does not matter for our purposes whether the Gomer in the text was an actual or symbolic wife for Hosea. Possessing the power of the Hebrew husband of his day, he could easily have exacted a vindictive justice. But we can imagine Hosea reflecting:

"It is true that my wife has been unfaithful. But in being unfaithful, even though she does not realize it yet, she has not only withdrawn from my love, but she is also entrusting herself to others who will take no responsibility for her. They will use her even as she is using them, simply for pleasure. This hurts me. But it is also her nature that is being subjected to strains it cannot take. She will be sooner or later defeated in her very attempt to attract admirers and convenient lovers. She will become older, less attractive, more desperate in her claims and more subject to victimization. She wants others to be responsive to and responsible for her, but she is unwilling to be responsive enough to the needs of others to accept responsibility for them. If I now put her away, if I add my punishment to the punishment that is already taking its toll of her nature, she will be hurt even more. Indeed, she will despise me with more justification for shutting her out of my life. Am I really doing justice to her by hurting her more and by hardening my own heart to her need? Can I encourage a relationship that will harden each of us against the other and make us even more vulnerable to our weaknesses? No, the intent of justice is to help her; I must be fair to the good in her as well as in me. I cannot do justice, actually, unless I love her steadfastly."

What has Hosea discovered through his own experience of himself and his total relation to his wife? The values of mercy and justice conflict if we do not understand their dynamics in human life. But full justice can never be done without mercy; and mercy cannot be authentic and reliable if it does not keep in mind both the good and the evil in a situation and if it does not work out a new relationship in which all involved can grow.

It may seem to some that this attempt to imagine and organize reflections in Hosea's mind (as a more or less unconscious seepage over a long period of experience) is making a great to-do about something as supposedly simple as love. But if "love" is a mere emotion having no relation to our experience and our thought, does it not fall low in the scale of values? On the other hand, if love is a life-style responsive to and responsible for the total growth of values in persons, values now actual and those which sensitive and realistic concern can bring into being, it can never be merely "sentiment" or "passion."

We shall need to elaborate on this statement later. But this much is already becoming clearer. *We cannot know what loving calls for apart from some guiding ideal of per-*

sonality, apart from some vision of what enables a human being to be a full person. Hence, it is not enough for John's parents to "love" him in order to bring him up properly. They must know what human beings—in this case a growing boy—are capable of, how it is possible to relate their potential powers to each other and to their total potential. But they must also have some idea of how to relate this total potential to the world of men and things. Neither is an easy task, and both are interrelated. A symphony of values, like an actual orchestra, must reflect more than the training and the complete musicianship of the individual players.

This Section is entitled "On Knowing God's Will." Yet I seem to have been talking only about finding and interrelating values in man. But my suggestion is that if we are to discover God's will *for man,* for the man God has created, we must examine man's nature to see what promotes and what discourages growth in the values God has made possible. God creates the conditions of growth, and I am convinced that without God neither the conditions nor the growth can be understood. I would also argue that all of our values take on special meaning when we live in the sense of God's presence with us in our actualizing of values.

But the basic point I wish to make here is that even if one does not believe in God, he cannot escape from the conditions for growth of values in personal life. If we are to know the human good, we must look for it in the values human nature actualizes as persons respond to other persons and to the universe in which they live. When men have disagreed about God's will they have always turned to their actual and possible value-experiences, including their religious experience, to help them to decide on a better course, or pattern of values, for their lives. There are other questions that come to mind, but some of them at least will be more adequately answered once it is clearer what is involved in realizing a pattern of values.

3 WHAT VALUES KEEP PERSONALITY GROWING?

The Values in Health, Truth, and Character

What elements, then, enter into John's prospective symphony of values? Obviously, the experience of health does. For health is an intrinsic value, and it is also instrumental to other values, in one's own life and in the lives of others. Here there seems to be no argument with John's parents. But even at this seemingly obvious starting point, we learn from experience to make a distinction between John's health and his comfort or bodily pleasures. Health maintains bodily efficiency, but many immediate bodily pleasures do not produce health.

The relationship between pleasure and other values is one of the most difficult to understand in every dimension of life. John is likely to think that if experiences are immediately pleasant they are, of course, good for him, or health-producing, until he learns from his own experience to sift out the bodily pleasures that are dependably related to his bodily health. Let John confuse comfort with health and he will become a self-indulgent boy with a lower capacity to resist illness than need be the case. The human body seems so made that the sacrifice of some plea-

45

sures and the endurance of some kinds of discomfort are necessary to the building and preserving of health.

But the health of a human body depends on so much more than being alive, or even having a strong constitution. Here if anywhere the interpenetration of values, or the mutual support necessary for the existence and growth in value-experience, is obvious. A human being cannot aim even at a "physical" value such as health without bringing into play two other realms of value, often distinguished as "spiritual": truth-values and character-values. Once alive, John can be healthy only in a society that has made it possible to discover the truth about the human body and is ready to pay the price for the good health of its citizens. And character-values come immediately to the fore: John himself must realize increasingly, as he grows older, that health is up to him. His doctor can prescribe, his parents can pay the costs, but John must take the medicine or learn to treat his body so as to be free of pills and doctor's bills.

"It all depends," we sometimes say, "upon a person's character." But what is character? And why, as this saying suggests, is it central in the search for values? Character is more than the more stable organization of a person's life. His character in this sense is the product, in good part at least, of a person's own willingness to discipline himself by the good or the ideal he acknowledges. To speak of *his* character is to speak literally of the "imprint" he makes upon his own personality as he matures. As we say, nobody else can build John's backbone for him. Parents, friends, and even enemies can create conditions that encourage him to discipline himself by what he believes to be good and true. But good intentions, all the truth in the world, will not in themselves bring him to sacrifice some goods for the sake of others, or accept some frustration and risk in order to realize the goals he accepts.

Even the discovery of truth, as well as the willingness to accept and apply it, requires character (in this sense). We forget that we can trust truth to be truth because someone who has had the character to develop in himself honesty and skill has accepted the responsibility for testing guesses by the ideals of verification. The most deceitful errors are those that parade as truth when they are at best half-truths. We simply cannot separate intellectual education from character formation—in this sense, as the person's willingness to guide himself by the ideal of truth. To discover the truth involves the patient willingness to test what seems true or false by the best evidence at hand and to put into practice the most reasonable conclusion.

In general, then, a person's character at a given point in his life is the shape that he has allowed his values, his ideals, and his actions to take.[1] John may be born with a strong body and a high intelligence, but what he does with each will depend on the specific character-values (such as honesty, courage, kindness, tolerance) he develops. These character values, each one a virtue, give more specific form to his total personality and outlook on life. We can now say: Man does not live by bread alone but by every virtue (character-value) that expresses the concrete meaning of self-discipline in the varied dimensions of life. There is no other way for a person to be creative in shaping the growth of values in his life or the directions his personality will take. And this is a fact about himself that he discovers but does not make, and it is one he cannot long deny without endangering the values he already has.

[1] Peter A. Bertocci and Richard M. Millard, *Personality and the Good* (New York: McKay, 1963), Chapters 16-17.

We must note another fact about truth and about character-values. Truth and character-values are not only indispensable to health in the human situation; they are not only indispensable to each other. They are also intrinsic values. Like health, they are enjoyed also for their own sake. This becomes clear when we ask ourselves: Suppose John were to have perfect physical health but was an idiot? The capacity to seek and know truth is not merely "basic to" human existence; it is a quality of a value experience that gives it meaning. Would we not prefer that John be able to risk his health, if need be, for the sake of knowing what it means to think and to search for truth? Is any thoughtful man willing to give up all the joys and the risks of truth-finding for the sake of health? But let us assume the impossible for the moment, that John is healthy and knows all the truth he needs. Yet if he never knew what it means to make the decisions that help create his own health or those necessary if truth is to be found and applied, would any of us envy him?

And now we realize that we have been taking another area of value-experience for granted. Suppose John did enjoy health and could, on the whole, master himself in the search for truth. Could he begin to appreciate what it means to be a person without enjoying his relationships to his fellow men? He must take at least one other step in value-realization.

What Do Affiliative Values Add?

The mutually supporting pattern of health, truth, and character-values has taken us far in our search for an ideal of personality. Every other venture in value will be affected by the degree to which these three are realized. Yet in the human situation, the development of each of these values is, in turn, closely related to another whole dimension of values, namely, the *affiliative*. Man may be a reason-capable animal, but his reasoning would not develop very much if he were not also a social animal. John's parents may know much about the conditions for his health, but they cannot afford to be ignorant of the importance of affiliative values for their offspring even in his infancy.

Most men come to realize that a living hell is a state of solitary confinement, or social ostracism and disapproval, with a total absence of companionship. Dostoevsky's criminal in *Crime and Punishment* finds himself cut off from society and then from family and friends. That is his punishment. John's parents have no more important task than to do their share in helping him see that the good life is the life with friends and for friends, an ever larger part of the human community that we take to ourselves. Even if John were healthy, brilliant, and strong-willed, a promising youth who could take care of himself and whose creative powers were bound to help others besides himself, to be unsocial would deprive him of the values of an innocent gregariousness. To live without smiles of cordiality, welcome, and approval or to be treated as if he were a thing and to treat others in this way, would be to poison the springs of his human well-being.

Even a 5-year-old boy seemed to understand the meaning of elementary human courtesy when he was reprimanded for not rising or making some appropriate remark of greeting when a guest came into the room. "I guess you

don't act in the same way when somebody walks into a
room as you would if you rolled in on your tricycle." One
always is a little suspicious of the motives of the "idealist"
who works for "man"—but does not enjoy men! Standing
alone is good only when it is for conscience's sake or for
God's sake, and then we are really suffering isolation for
the sake of a richer or larger communion for which we
stand "in conscience."

In the light of human need for growth in affiliative responsiveness, we can better understand why it is that the
son of the surgeon, who took no interest in his son for
himself, was living in a "well-furnished psychological
slum." Many parents are so interested in bringing up their
children for the "higher values" that they seem to forget
that no family will ever be a home without "just being
glad to be together." To be born of human beings, nur-
tured in a family, to play and work with one's peers, and
never really to be able to do without the friendly response
of others—this is the inescapable human situation. This is
why every other value in life, including sex, is affected by
what we do with our affiliative potential. The first order of
human business is to relate one's own values and potential
to the values and potential of others. We cannot say we
love God while treating our neighbor as if he could not
love or be loved by either God or man!

Health, truth, character, and affiliative values—these are
experiences that human beings must enjoy for their own
sake. But they must also discover the relations of these
values to one another in their own lives and in the lives of
others. We now begin to glimpse what it means to talk
about an ideal of personality, a symphony of values. The
symphony of values is a pattern of mutually supportive

values creative of a maximum width and depth in one's own life in relation to the lives of others. Each of the values we have been discussing expresses a dimension of human existence in its dependence on the environment, social and non-social, surrounding it. We need still to sketch out these dimensions of value-experience: the economic, the vocational, the aesthetic, and the holy.

Economic Value: Work

A person's *work* is the task he performs in order to sustain himself in his environment. Work is a fact of life for most of us, and that man is happy who can turn the fact into a value, not merely an instrumental necessity for survival but a source of intrinsic satisfaction. Persons spend most of their waking time at their work, and the quality of their health, character, and affiliative values is affected by their work. What happens at work will influence not only the part John will play in the community and in the family but also constitute a persistent core in his sense of personal significance. If John and his wife cannot share their work, be it at the shop or in the home, they may well find themselves isolated from each other; and they may lose an important source of affiliative values in their lives. The surgeon and his wife (see above p. 4) began to lose each other because of their attitude toward each other's work. If we turn rather abruptly to the value of *vocation*, it is not to minimize the importance of economic activities, but to explore a problem that every person faces both in relation to work and to other values.

The Value of Vocation

"Vocation" is very hard to define, but the lack of it can be detected when a person, whether before or after he has achieved economic competence, feels that his life does not count for anything. We all know persons of whom we might say: "He's a good boy," "He means well, but . . ." This kind of person breaks no windows, but neither does he let in the light; he does not complain, but neither is he willing to help make conditions better for others. He is "like a lot of other people" simply because there is nowhere he really wants to go. His upbringing has kept him from any serious evil, and he is accommodating and "congenial," but we feel that he himself knows that he isn't getting anywhere.

It would be easy to say that I am talking about character and affiliative values again. For neither parents nor society can give him a sense of vocation any more than they can give him character-values or make his human relations meaningful. Vocation is a matter of outlook, of self-evaluation affected by social evaluation, and it can reach into religious concern. A person with a sense of vocation is directed by a purpose that makes life worthwhile, at least for himself. Something is worth doing, and his own life acquires worth as he commits himself. In such action he may feel himself a significant part of a larger social group that, he believes, needs his help. Or he may initiate a project that challenges him and for whose success he is willing to sacrifice.

Few experiences give more tone to inner life than this sense of vocation; and few become more easily the stimulus to further effort and growth. Thus, a sense of vocation is a commitment to what one does that can be aroused by, and initiates, other loves. As we shall see, "falling in love" can mean falling into a sense of vocation, for now one's life has an all-embracing aim. We have urged that if love is to grow its vocation must include the home and the family (or its equivalents). Again, if a young man and a young woman "in love" see their work in relation to their marriage, they have been promoted from job to vocation.

A sense of vocation seems to spring from a vision of the creative possibilities in any task or course of action. "Vocation" (the word's origin in Latin suggests "being called to") inspires and is inspired by a sense of purpose. Like the sun, it burns away the fog of aimlessness, the mere doing of one thing after another that makes life at best a dead routine. The sense of vocation is important, then, because it can transform an assortment of value-experiences into a mutually sustaining pattern of values unified by a purpose. Indeed, the sense of vocation is the sense of *personal significance.* And the sense of personal significance grows in one as he feels that he is important for what he is and can be to others.

Again, as we shall see, this is why "being loved" can give one this sense of personal significance. When there is no personal significance in love it ceases to be love even if the word is used. But the sense of personal significance can be no greater than the values being "centered," unified, and developed. Alas, life can be "interesting" but never centered, as the person who is always looking for interesting experiences illustrates. For a person's significance is rooted in the kinds of values his life organizes, and the promising organization of values is toward some goal that challenges to further growth.

Indeed, what is brought out by the maxim: "Love God and do as you please!" is the fact that there must be a center of worship that transcends, even as it gives selective focus to, the values experienced. In minimal terms, whatever a person values, whatever values inform his daily experience must take root and challenge his potential as a person *in his total situation;* he must have a sense of his importance in his whole situation as he sees it; otherwise, even sacrifice is meaningless. If vocation in this larger sense of personal significance suggests religion, it is not surprising. And if the emphasis on organization of values suggests the art of living, we are simply being reminded again of the interpenetration of values in our lives. But the place of art and aesthetic values constitutes an area of experience easy to misconstrue in its relation to other values, so we must pause for a fresh look.

Aesthetic Value: The Force of Beauty

In their effort to guide the growth of their son, John's parents will be passing though a country that has sometimes been called the "realm of beauty." It is a peculiarly deceptive land; on the surface, it promises easy pleasure, while beneath the surface, it is mined by explosive forces. Of this John's parents may become aware on the day, if not earlier, that John reveals what they call "puppy love" or a "crazy infatuation" for a girl who, in their view, may be "pretty" or even "beautiful" but has few or none of the qualities that would make a good wife for their son. And they find themselves confronted with the dreadful possibility that all their labors may be nullified by their son's marriage to "that woman"!

Beauty, then, is a force, and we ignore this fact at our peril. As I shall indicate later, no understanding of the power of sex and love is possible to us if we neglect the force of beauty in them. Thus, John may find that power in the relation of the parts of a girl's features—eyes, nose, mouth, chin, brow, shape of the head, texture and glow of the skin. Though his parents keep reminding him that "beauty is skin-deep," it may become one of his leading motives for marriage.

What is this "force"? It is that intrinsic something in the organization of a human body or a mountain, of a novel or a sonnet, even of a paragraph of nonfiction prose, that will make us stop short in delight or wonder and ask for a second look or a second hearing. And even when we become quite familiar with the "facts" of a face or landscape or the information and ideas in a piece of writing, we find ourselves returning again and again to the object of such delight. We "put it on again," as in the case of a record that transcribes this same kind of effect in the relation of sounds. The source of this delight or wonder we can only partly explain; after all our explanations, as in the case of a musical recording, we must have recourse to putting the record on so that, as we say, it may explain itself. Actually, it explains very little, and that is why John despairs of ever conveying to his parents "what he sees in that girl."

Beauty, in a word, is an elemental mystery and force; and as in the case of all such forces, it can be controlled and refined and won to the idea of a "symphony" of values. But it cannot be suppressed without dwarfing a personality. As Emerson likes to remind us, men prefer to receive their truth and their morals in the form of beauty. They will always give anything beautifully said or done "more of a break" than it deserves in the eyes of the narrow moralist and the narrow philosopher. It is hard to exclude "aesthetic quality" (to use a more exact phrase) from any

aspect of experience; our very phrase *"symphony* of values" describes not only how mutually supportive and unified values can be, but it also glories aesthetically in the
fact.

John's parents, accordingly, will do well to reflect that
we use the word *fine* in, for example, a "fine figure"
(where the reference is to physical relationships), "fine
feeling" (where the reference is to an emotional response), "fine act" (where the reference is to conduct), or
"fine book" (where the reference is at least partly to what
kind and quality of knowledge the book contains). In
bringing John up, if they keep in mind the aesthetic factor
in their son's makeup, instead of talking solely about
John's "duty" to do such and such a thing, they will ask
him sometimes if "it would not be a fine thing to do." And
certainly, when they seek to prevail upon him to do well
any task he undertakes and to "finish the job," they will
have better success if John has developed a liking for parts
of high quality that fit together very well and form a
whole. As Leibniz so well expressed it: "If our eyes could
see the beauty of virtue, we should love it warmly."

In this pervasive area of aesthetic values, John's parents
will find methods of guidance especially elusive. Of course,
they will encourage him to do his art work in grammar
school, perhaps take courses in art or art history later on;
they will seek to provide good pictures, good records, trips
to galleries and museums; they will raise the funds for
theater and concert. Yet here, perhaps more than in other
areas, example counts most. A work of art is never really
born from a theory; it is born from another work of art
even when it seems to react against it. For John, it is the
atmosphere of the home, intellectual, moral, artistic and
religious, that will be seeping into his pores and fibers;

he will probably learn more from fine manners and morals in fine people than from sermons and ethical treatises. Everywhere, without being aware of it, he will be searching for images of thought and feeling, of action and reverence, upon which he will unconsciously model himself, just as he adopts unconsciously the carriage and manner of his favorite hero. Here, more than in other areas of his education, his parents will seek to expose John naturally to the best examples and leave his education to the human tendency to grow in the image of what is loved. They know that his life needs to "build something," that in some sense it will have to be "poetry in action" if it is ever itself to become a *vocation*.

We have been trying to put into words the kind of difference that aesthetic response makes to a life. Any of us who have felt its force know that it has its own way of transforming and "opening life up." We cannot restrict it to any one phase of life, and yet we know that we feel its power in some experiences more than in others; and sometimes we idolize these experiences. As we turn to the value in religion, we shall find it even more difficult to be accurate and brief; but we know that any attempt to speak of transforming experiences as well as depth responses must not neglect consideration of the place of religious experience.

Religious Value: Creativity in Ultimate Faith

Into the mouth of Joan of Arc, Maxwell Anderson puts the words: "Sometimes people believe in little or nothing; nevertheless they give up their lives for that little or nothing . . . But to surrender what you are and live without belief—that's more terrible than dying—more terrible than dying young."[2] Something like this was suggested in our discussion of *vocation*. But it is important not to identify the religious quest with the sense of vocation, much as the two may seem to be, or become, one in a given personality. A person can have a sense of vocation, he may enjoy a profound sense of significance without any religion—unless we stretch the word *religion* to mean any far-reaching commitment, such as his job or his marriage. I wish simply to emphasize that many strong and inspiring persons have had a sense of purpose or vocation to which they would not apply the word *religious*. I do not wish to impose the word on them and I would also argue that such persons are correct in identifying themselves as nonreligious.

In keeping with the mainstream of great religions and great religious persons, I shall define an experience or a value as religious[3] if, in and through it, the person feels or believes he is linked up to whatever he holds to be the unifying Source of value in man and nature, and yet is neither man nor nature as ordinarily defined. A religious man, in these terms, is one who worships the Source of values (or what he conceives to be the Being upon whom everything ultimately depends, however that dependence is finally defined by him). I am not arguing the question

[2] Maxwell Anderson, *Joan of Lorraine*, in *Three Plays*, edited and with Introduction by George Freedley (New York: Washington Square Press, 1962), p. 89. Copyright 1947 by Maxwell Anderson. All rights reserved. Reprinted by permission of Anderson House.

[3] See, for three different interpretations of religious experience, H. D. Lewis, *Philosophy of Religion* (London: The English Universities Press, 1965); Abraham Maslow, *Religion, Values, Peak-Experiences* (Columbus: The Ohio State University Press, 1964); and Paul Tillich, *The Courage to Be* (New Haven: Yale University Press, 1952) and *Dynamics of Faith* (New York: Harper, 1957).

whether God exists, or whether any particular kind of God exists (for example, God as person). But I am providing the background for the assertion that a religious man is a man whose sense of vocation is dominated by his belief in, and worship of, God.[4]

I hold, then, that if a person can set at the center of his life the worship of God as the inspiring force of all his value-experience, his whole existence takes on a quality and creative power no other kind of experience can give. I would want to argue further that if a person can believe that God cares for him for his own sake, that God, as the Judeo-Christian faith conceives Him, has involved Himself and does involve Himself in the creation of all persons at every point in their development, he has a vision that can release transforming and creative power of the highest order. For now he believes that creativity-in-love is the underlying source and goal in his own life and in the universe. And his own search for an inclusive and yet creative pattern of values becomes part of the cosmic drama in which other persons and God are to be respected even as they inspire and challenge his own search for value.

Having expressed my own ultimate conviction, I need hardly add that in every era there are good men convinced that this faith—and any like it—is not only unfounded but breeds immaturity. In my own youth, and since, I have found the following passage from Walter Lippmann an eloquent challenge. Speaking for many through the centuries and in our day, Mr. Lippmann says:

[4] In *Introduction to the Philosophy of Religion* (New York: Prentice-Hall, 1951), Chapters 1, 12-18, I have elaborated on the whole problem; and I have put the argument in the most elementary way I know how in *Why Believe in God?* (New York: Association Press, 1963), using *Religion as Creative Insecurity* (New York: Association Press, 1959) to express what I suggest as the norm of religious growth.

A boy can take you into the open at night and show
you the stars; he might tell you no end of things
about them, conceivably all that an astronomer could
teach. But until and unless he feels *the vast indifference of the universe to his own fate,* and has placed
himself in the perspective of cold and illimitable
space, he has not looked maturely at the heavens.
*Until he has felt this, and unless he can endure this,
he remains a child,* and in his childishness he will
resent the heavens when they are not accommodating.[5]

Obviously, Mr. Lippmann's definition of "maturity" is
affected by his conviction that the universe is vastly in-
different to man's fate. He who believes that the love of a
Creator and creative God abides in the stars and is the final
source of his own yearning for creativity in love will find
maturity in his deeper sense of responsibility for the creation of values in God's world. One's religious commitment
—and the above are not, of course, the only choices—will
involve every other value in his life, suffuse his way of
looking at himself and his neighbor, and, as we saw in the
first chapter, his attitude toward the meaning of a home. It
is my own conviction that in sex, love, marriage, and home
a human being can feel resonance to the reality of God's
love in his experience. God is not "added" to his experi-

---

[5] Walter Lippmann, *A Preface to Morals,* p. 187. My italics. (Reprinted
with permission of The Macmillan Company, New York. Copyright 1929
by Walter Lippmann, renewed 1957 by Walter Lippmann.) Contrast with
this Kant's witness (in the "Conclusion" to his *Critique of Practical Reason,*
translated and edited by Lewis Beck White [Chicago: University of Chicago Press, 1949], p. 258): "Two things fill the mind with ever new and
increasing admiration and awe, the oftener and more steadily they are re-
flected on: the starry heavens above me and the moral law within me."

ence any more than love and marriage are "added" to sex.
They are mutually involved in the sensitive search for the
best in value-experience.

Yet a person may come to the point where he feels he
must settle for indifference as a principle of life. I would
wish only to question that he is the more "mature" in
these matters because he has settled for it. I am aware of
the terrible things men have done in the name of God, but
I cannot believe it is mature to turn our back on great
spirits who have changed the history of man because their
religious quest ended with a God whose relation to them
inspired worshiping love and selfless and yet self-fulfilling
creativity.

Whatever the final truth in the matter, each person
must find his way. I wish only to emphasize that the religious quest, like the quest for truth, for beauty, for community, must remain incomplete. Even so, it rewards with
moments of peculiar joy and power; and even its despairs
are never meaningless. We need not expect the heavens to
accommodate themselves to us, but we do need to ask
whether the order and beauty that they symbolize have any
relation to the order and beauty to which our own human
lives aspire. Hence, I find the words of the psychologist
Gordon W. Allport a more adequate expression of the
mature religious sentiment:

> The adult mind, provided that it is still growing,
> stretches its rational capacities as far as it can with the
> logic of induction, deduction, and a weighing of
> probabilities. While the intellect continues to exert
> itself, the individual finds that he needs to build
> aspiring defenses against the intellect's almost certain
> failure. He learns that to surmount the difficulties of

a truculent world he needs also faith and love. Thus
religion, engaging as it does reason, faith, and love,
becomes for him morally true. Most religious people
claim that it is also metaphysically true because they
feel that outer revelation and mystical experience
have brought them supernatural assurance. Thus the
warrant for certitude comes from the total orienta-
tion that the person attains in his quest for a comprehensive belief-system capable of relating him to existence as a whole.[6]

There can be mature belief in God and mature unbelief. But there will be no maturity in value-creativity for
him who spurns the quest. The finest tribute a man can
pay to the deepest value-experience is to be tempted to see
its objective glory mirrored in the stars. "Maturity" may
come, in the face of this temptation, in a "yes"; it may
come in a "no." One may doubt that it will ever come to
that young man who, without finding out for himself
where his very self and its meaning are at stake, never lives
deeply enough to face the problem of creative belief or
creative unbelief.

But assuming a "yes" to the religious quest, we must
realize that the religious dimension of human existence,
since it involves the affiliative, the theoretical, and the
moral, cannot thrive in isolation from the other dimensions. Religious experience needs the criticism and the
support that it can gain from the rest of value-experience;
indeed, it needs all the rest of a person's value-experience
to give it further point and broader relevance to the
growth of the whole person.

[6] G. W. Allport, *Becoming* (New Haven: Yale University Press, 1960),
p. 95.

Growth in Values: An Unfinished Symphony

We have come to the end of our effort to trace, however sketchily, a basic pattern of values in personality. My suggestion is that without some such pattern we can give no concrete meaning to the words *person, maturity* and *love.* To love myself is to fulfill my potential in value-experiences. But these will take me beyond themselves and beyond myself as I discover that there can be no health-values without character-values, and without truth-values and affiliative-values, and so on. And what can it mean to love another concretely unless I join with him in this search for values that will do no unnecessary violence to his potential?

To love another is to care for his existence in health, for his ventures in truth-finding, self-control, social concern, vocation, aesthetic and religious experience. Love links two persons because they grow together *and* in individuality in their search for values which, they discover, do form a pattern or network. It is the very nature of love, because it is the very nature of persons, to be both conservative and creative. For when persons build they begin where they are, save what they can as they move to new forms and levels of health, human sensitivity, truth, and creative control in value-experiences. Love always has work to do because it is always on the frontier of a personality, protecting the rear as it ventures into new, risky, but promising territory. Love knows the meaning of "be ye wise as serpents, but gentle as doves." For it cannot simply accept any *status quo;* it accepts in order to push on to another level or another dimension of value without forgetting past and present strength and weakness.

In view of what has been said, it may be clear that this pattern of values is not suggested by, or grounded in, social convention or mores. Of course each person lives with other persons and his growth is affected by them and their levels of value. But value-experiences are the experiences of persons with themselves and with other persons in their total environment. They are not the product of custom, but they suggest customs and they challenge customs when customs seem to destroy them.

The so-called moral revolution in sex is the attempt of persons to challenge "what has been said and done" for the sake of increasing value-experiences in sex and love when new biological knowledge and other changes in the environment seem to open up new possibilities for value-experience. But is the value-experience of sex as a personal experience in a class by itself? Hardly. The problem is to protect its value in the life of persons and to increase its value. The problem is also is to ask whether persons in "making love" without loving do in fact find that even their emotions dry up so that what appears for a while is an embalmed body in a casket—a body that may look like a person even though the heart no longer beats. Customs and even laws begin to totter the moment enough persons feel that their own authentic experiences of value, their own authentic heartbeats, are being killed and their lives poured into caskets with a ritual that has no vitality for them.

A word of warning is in order. I have been urging that we respect both freedom and order, both openness and stability in personality. Human nature is very flexible, and each person in his combination of attitudes, needs, abilities, and values will always be unique. Any pattern of values will always have to take form in accordance with a particular developing nature. The pattern of values is a guideline and not a stencil, a mold, or a Procrustean bed! We do not decide whether John is to be a doctor at his birth; likewise, we cannot determine how the specific pattern of values will best work out in his life.

The concrete art of living weaves in a groping way a fabric of values that seeks, as far as possible, an equilibrium in motion. At every point the problem is to keep values both sustaining one another and creating the conditions for new developments. I call this pattern a *symphony* of values in order to emphasize the importance of orchestrating value-themes in a particular life so that a mutually sustaining, dynamic, self-fulfilling, self-challenging harmony will result. The life good to live is never static; it is never just a collection of parts. It is always infused by a larger theme (vocation and religion). It will have a grace and beauty of its own as it works out that theme more comprehensively as well as more intensively. Hence, the image of an *unfinished symphony* will express the mutual process in human life where dynamic supportive elements continually face the threat of maintaining themselves and growing in the face of discordant elements.

Furthermore, in any person (in any partnership, in any society or state), development or realization in value-experiences will be uneven, simply because persons cannot do everything at once, and because mistakes are made—as well as for a host of unavoidable causes. The problem each person faces is that of realizing the best that lies in him as a person. There are symphonies and symphonies, just as there are themes and themes. No symphony will be greater than its themes; yet the themes will be worked out as themes of a symphony.

Our concern in the rest of this book is with the themes

that begin in the sexual sensitivity of a person. It is not an
artificial theme, and every person must decide how that
theme will be woven into his total search for values. There
are unique values this theme contributes, and the problem
is to be adequately sensitive to them and to the problems
a person confronts in weaving them into what must be for
him always an unfinished symphony.

The Unfinished Symphony and Marriage

The experience of two young people may help to illustrate what happens when persons marry and discover that
they have not been clear enough about the values which
they themselves hold and upon which they depend to keep
their love growing.

Sallie, a very attractive girl with an engaging personality, was brought up in the Southwest. Her father and
mother were sturdy and convinced Christians, persuaded
that the Bible is the infallible word of God, convinced that
the Christian has a responsibility to his community and to
the underprivileged, black or white, yet unwilling to move
on a wide social scale to improve the lot of the Negro
even though they were actively engaged in helping promising Negroes to go to good private schools and colleges.

Sallie's own experience in college involved her in questioning what she now believed were extremely conservative religious and social attitudes. She no longer believed
in an infallible Bible, and she thought that the path of
practical Christian wisdom lay in enabling the Negro to
find better housing, schooling, and employment, provided
that violence was avoided. By temperament and habit she
did not like large groups and believed that social change

should not move faster than leadership responsible to the whole community. She was an avid reader, loved art, believed in the church, and looked forward to a family in which she could become a homemaker. In her junior year in college she went to a summer school in the North and met the man whom she was to marry a year later after her graduation.

Henry, Sallie's husband, had (as she described him) all the firmness and integrity of her father. He was an alert young man now in the midst of his doctoral work in a social science. When she married him he seemed like the person who would be sufficiently complementary to her own growth. "Henry had lots of positive ideas not only about science but about changing the world, and he was good at expressing them."

Once they were fairly well convinced that they might be married, Henry made it clear that he saw no reason why they, using contraceptive precautions, should not have premarital sexual intercourse. While Sallie "would have preferred not to, I thought my attitudes on this subject probably had not changed enough, and since I intended to marry him, I decided to give in, because it seemed to mean so much to him." During this period before marriage they lived on widely separated campuses, so their intercourse was as occasional as their meetings, but, as she said, "for me it was enjoyable enough," and he was satisfied.

Here then were two healthy young people with common aesthetic interests, who cared about other people, had enough economic security, and believed in broad educational pursuits. They had vocational interests that were not conflicting and yet gave unity to each life, and their sexual experience indicated no basic disharmony in that respect. What they did not talk about much was their attitude toward God and the part religion should play in life. Sallie had passed off the difference she sensed as due to his scientific attitude which "I could live with, since he seemed to care about people."

What then brought her, two years after marriage, to such pervasive unhappiness and general anxiety that she did not believe she could go on with their marriage? Indeed, he had asked her to consider suing for a divorce.

I am not so much interested here in the final truth or falsity of the description she gave as I am in her own perception of the situation. What comes out clearly is that the values we discussed above, which may have seemed like a bloodless pattern of abstractions, are dynamic factors when we see their interplay in a specific life and in two young people who do not doubt that love will conquer all as they marry.

For Sallie religious experience was vivid and strong, but she was not apt in the rational defense of the dogmas of her faith. She found her husband increasingly contemptuous of her beliefs and disparaging of her willingness to go on holding them if she could not give "good reasons" for believing them. He had given up his childhood faith because he could not prove God's existence in a way that was consistent with his scientific standards. Furthermore, as he saw it, people who believed in God were so intolerant and self-righteous that they opposed social progress. For him the fact that Sallie and her folks were sensitive to the plight of the underprivileged as well as professing and dedicated Christians was nullified by their unwillingness to take massive steps in improving the state of the Negro. Since she was not good at verbalizing her convictions, she came to dread the occasions when these matters came up for discussion, when scorn and ridicule took the place of reason.

Matters did not improve when he carried on in the same way when friends were invited in for the evening. "He is interested in the masses, he wants to 'change the system,' but he has fewer human relations with the underprivileged, white or black, than I do."

It is worth noting in passing that here are two people who care for others but in different ways, she in the name of a conservatively conceived Christian God, he in the name of scientific truth and humanism. He was more interested in social changes that would induce improvement, but he had little immediate sympathy and concern for the people around him. She did not appreciate the importance of the social conditions affecting the lives of persons, but was involved in community concerns both in and outside of the church. He felt that her Christian motivation was unreasonable and in any case too conservative in social terms; she felt that for him people became pawns that should be moved around. Even this interpretation oversimplifies, I am sure, the specific ways in which these convictions actually operated in the lives of these two persons, but we see how their way of conceiving the truth and their attitudes toward God, the church, and the problems of the underprivileged actually separated them because they both took their convictions seriously. Her friends, to whom she increasingly looked for warmth, were in the church; his were more like him in their attitude to her, and she found entertaining them an uncomfortable chore.

But another factor had come into play even before these latent differences came into the open. Very soon after their marriage, partly owing to ill-health on Sallie's part, they had found their sexual intercourse emotionally inadequate. Sallie said that it was her fault, that she found it almost impossible to be properly responsive, that she increasingly found "these other things" made it hard to be "really self-giving" because she felt more "manipulated" than "cared for." In any case, at the time of our interview, they had gone on for a number of months with no intercourse, largely because he had given up trying and "I guess I'm trying too hard to come up to his expectations."

This couple provide a very good case for different psychotherapeutic approaches. That is not what concerns me here. The fact is that, as each partner perceived the situation, a clash of values different from any anticipated was influencing the specific quality of this marriage and even the quality of the sexual experience and its place in their lives. These young people were finding that their marriage brought out latent but important differences in their outlook on life, and—what is more—that these differences in value had become so dominant that they now threatened the continuance of the marriage.

But why had Sallie even now come to talk rather than proceed with arrangements for a divorce? "I know I've made mistakes, and have allowed many resentments to overcome me at times, but after all, as a Christian I believe in forgiveness, and I just cannot quit yet." I felt that they both needed more help than I could give and made recommendations, although Sallie did not think that Henry felt he needed counselling. What is clear is that there is a Christian basis in her life for a self-critical patience that can lead to a more successful mutual relationship (assuming that her perception of herself and Henry is basically correct). It was not clear that his total outlook would allow him to be sufficiently repentant and forgiving to move to a deeper understanding.

After two years of marriage Sallie and Henry have come to the parting of the ways and need to discover what they *now* are willing to work for—and love for—together. Their problem is not money, social position, health, but basic interpretation of their attitudes toward truth-finding, toward each other and other people, and toward the meaning of God. Their individual symphonies of values are far from unfinished, but the way in which they are willing to work together for each other and with respect for their disliked differences will be critical. We return then to our fundamental theme.

A marriage and a home is never more than what two persons bring to it. It is impossible to overestimate the importance of the specific value-patterns that keep persons growing or prevent their growth. To marry another person is to marry the value-pattern which gives direction to his being. Our thesis is that in our day it has become all the more important for us to become aware and articulate about the kind of human beings we ought to become. Decisions about particular issues, such as sex and marriage, cannot be adequate unless we keep the person as a whole, and persons-in-relation, in mind.

In the remainder of this book we shall be asking what policy should govern our thinking and acting about sex if its own value is to be enhanced and if it is to be a creative factor in the unfinished symphony of values.

4 DISCOVERING THE ROLE OF SEX IN PERSONALITY

The Biomorphic Conception of Sex and Man

It would be much easier to evaluate sex if sexual activities performed only one role in a person's life. Uncritical assumptions about sex have cost persons of both sexes much needless frustration and suffering.

A student said recently: "I have learned from biology that man is a biological creature like any other animal. I'm convinced that it is foolish to put sexual restrictions upon him. If you go too far in asking people to control their sexual desire, you are simply putting unnatural inhibitions in the way of their happiness. You can't push these desires back too far and too long any more than you can keep from eating and drinking."

Even if the student's biology is correct—is biology really the place to find a full picture of man?—there is another serious assumption here. How does he define, how does he know what is "too far" and "too long"? Without realizing it, he has gone from biology to ethics, from what he thinks man is like to what he thinks men ought to be. How do we decide how much persons ought to eat and drink, granted their need? The preceding chapter was an attempt to show

73

that man *as a person* has many dimensions to his being, and that there is no answer as easy as the one this student seemed to have in mind.

The fact is that once we have said that sex is the biological basis for human reproduction, there is very little else upon which we can find universal agreement among the informed. The co-authors of *Human Sexual Response,* Dr. William H. Masters and Virginia E. Johnson, develop a distinction that supports the suggestion here. They leave no doubt that the physiological sexual response is only one dimension of sex. "Sex is easy enough to define. It's harder to pinpoint sexuality. Perhaps we can say that sexuality is the dimension of personality that gains its impetus from the reproductive drive."[1]

It is clear that for Masters and Johnson the development of sexuality involves the meaning and the value of sex in the personality. They write, for example:

Whether we are sexual people from birth, simply by virtue of having been born male and female, or whether we "learn" sexuality early in infancy is a moot point that psychologists and psychiatrists will continue to debate. But what is absolutely clear is that sexuality does not suddenly emerge at puberty, that it is not born of glandular change or the ability to reproduce. Sexuality is the quality of living as a sexually motivated being. This qualitative factor of human personality remains an influence, whether it is sublimated in a condition of celibacy or continually expressed in an on-going sexual relationship.[2]

[1] Dr. William H. Masters and Virginia E. Johnson, "A Defense of Love and Morality," in *McCall's* (November, 1966), p. 102.
[2] *Ibid.,* p. 173.

And, stressing the importance of an education for responsibility, rather than mere do's and don'ts, they recommend:

> Somewhere between the ages of twelve and sixteen a youngster needs to know your value system about the relationship between men and women. He needs to know that there are ways in which men and women exploit each other's sexuality and ways in which they honor it.[3]

We cannot even say that in any one person the sexual response is of necessity directed solely to members of the opposite sex. Indeed, had we not made the mistake of assuming that our children would necessarily become heterosexual, fewer of them would probably have become homosexual!

In our day, we need to be aware of the kind of assumptions we are making about the nature of man and the potential of sex. We have suffered much and still suffer from what I shall call the *biomorphic* conception of sex in human life. This belief may be somewhat crudely put thus: "You don't have to teach children or adolescents about sex; since the sexual pattern of response is built into a human being, by the time they are married, male and female will know what to do in order to procreate. There is very little you can do about sex before a human being is physically ready; after he is physically ready, the 'instinct' to procreate is so strong in the species that you are just going against nature to expect a human being to control himself or herself. It's almost like asking a hungry or thirsty person not to eat or drink."

[3] *Ibid.*

Some statement of this sort, I believe, would describe what many of us tend to think about sex. Sex, because it is connected with procreation, is so strong a physiological urge in human nature that you invite defeat if you try to curb it. I call this view *biomorphic* since it regards sex as essentially a biological drive that must be treated as one would treat any other strong physical need; namely, we must understand it for what it is and deal with it only as we deal with any other physical function—keep it from hurting anyone physically—and then let it alone to function "naturally."

How the Biomorphic View Influences Thinking About Chastity

A *biomorphic ethics* develops readily from this biomorphic view of sex. A consistent proponent might urge: Let us teach our children all they need to know about the physiology of sex. Let this teaching be done carefully, with children of both sexes, so that they will be able to assimilate the facts as they grow older. They should know how babies come and what measures can be taken, healthy and unhealthy, to prevent conception. With proper delicacy— since we are dealing with a complicated physiological mechanism—but firmly and accurately, we must provide the information required to keep persons healthy in their sexual functioning.

Now I certainly do not deny the importance of this biomorphic dimension. I need not stop to underscore the importance in home, school, and church of appropriate sex informaton for children, adolescents, and adults. No adequate ethics of sex can be built on misconceptions of what the physiological facts about sex and procreation are. But our dependence on this dimension has been more extensive than we realized. For example, have we not in fact based much of our argument against premarital sexual intercourse on biomorphic contentions? We may have had other considerations in mind, but we felt we were on safer ground when we told our children that premarital intercourse was bad because it could lead to venereal disease and to unwanted pregnancy.

Indeed, the double standard of sexual morality stemmed in good part from biomorphic thinking. Why expect men, who are different from women physiologically (and whose sexual responsiveness is presumed to be much greater), to control their very strong, natural desire? Sound medical advice could keep men from venereal disease, and they could take proper precautions not to become fathers. Women (who presumably were not so sexually responsive) were expected to remain virgins and not take any risks of becoming mothers out of wedlock.

The all-important consideration from this point of view was to keep men and women in separate roles, largely dictated by physiological and presumed sexual differences. Women simply had to accept the responsibilities and hardships that went with their biological role as mothers, just as men had to prepare themselves for their essential responsibility as breadwinners and soldiers. Everything seems so clear and nicely partitioned in this biomorphic view, even if the logic is dubious and the "facts" are fictions. A man who before marriage felt free to reduce the number of virgins available insisted upon a virgin as his mate in matrimony. The woman who yielded to a man's presumably irresistible urge was either a "bad" woman or belonged to that despised (though useful) category of females called prostitutes. It was important to distinguish the virgin when one married.

Contraceptives as Undermining the Physiological Grounds for Chastity

Even though the prevalence of venereal disease is still startling, especially because of its appearance among adolescents, informed persons can avail themselves of medical aids to prevent it or cure it. One fact that probably led to a questioning of sexual codes is that thousands of the veterans returning from World War II had already learned the proper use of prophylactics. No effective case against premarital intercourse can be based any longer on the fear of venereal disease and its consequences.

The advent of virtually foolproof contraceptives is a formidable threat to the physiological grounds for chastity. A doctor carried out the logic of this view when he asked school authorities not to interfere with his daughter's rights to sexual self-expression, because he had provided her with proper protection against the possibility of pregnancy. And middle-class prudence took this form: "After all, I have put too much into my daughter's education to take any chances of her becoming pregnant owing to some unexpected turn of events on the evening of the senior prom. I have seen to it that our doctor provides her with the best contraceptive aid modern science can give her."

Why should this hard-nosed biological logic escape a coed who, in writing a paper on this whole problem, put one side of the issue effectively by posing four questions: "First, if intercourse is possible without pregnancy, what's wrong with it, if no one is being hurt? Second, since marriage is only a means of preventing illegitimate children [note the view of marriage], contraceptives should enable everyone to have intercourse without bothering about marriage. Third, if two persons found themselves incompatible in bed, they could discover this beforehand and thus avoid divorce. Indeed, if one has had previous intercourse, is one not less likely to be awkward and be a poor partner, especially on the honeymoon and the earlier days of marriage? Fourth, now that we women are in a supposedly equal society with men, why shouldn't both sides make the rules, especially since women now can avoid pregnancy?"

Once the thoroughly biomorphic view of sex and marriage is accepted as a premise, it seems impossible to deny the conclusions based upon it. Thus the young lady in question wisely shifted to nonbiological aspects of the question. My own experience in the past twenty-five years, with collegiate and noncollegiate young people, testifies to their perplexity as to the relation of the biological and other consequences of premarital intercourse to the good life in marriage. Since they have been brought up on the biomorphic case (which is easiest to present and understand) against premarital sexual intercourse and now can no longer see the biological grounds for self-denial, they often decide that their sexual conscience has become outmoded. They come to feel that the restraints of conscience are nothing but inhibitions pressed upon them by parents in a society that has earlier faced a different biological and social situation. Under changed circumstances, aren't their feelings of guilt a cultural lag, a hangover from different conditions? Why should the horse-and-buggy scheme of traffic still be relevant to an automotive age, especially when one has safety belts? Why, indeed, if the only case for premarital chastity and even for marriage is a biomorphic one?

Man: Not a Higher Animal But a Person

Why is the biomorphic view of sex inadequate? Because a human being is a person, and his sexuality must be understood as a part of his life as a person. Nor should we be misled by the phrase, "Man is a higher animal." It does not mean that human experience can be reduced to that of the highest animal. Even those who take the biomorphic view remind us that the expression of sex in human beings is much more variable than the relatively fixed ways of expression in animals. If nothing else could make us aware of the difference between man and animal, a swift comparison of the symphony of values with the values which even the highest animal can experience should be decisive.

To be specific, what do we have in mind when we affirm that a human being is a person, and how does this affect our thinking about sex? To say that *a person can sense, desire, remember, imagine, perceive, will, think, be responsive morally, aesthetically, and religiously* is to make a mere beginning. Among other things, this means that he can be aware that he is active in these ways. He is a self-conscious being. And, as self-conscious, he is able to analyze the quality of his experiences, compare them to one another, and then trace their relationship to each other. Even if a person's urges, emotions, and feelings could be said to be "animal," they would be transformed by the fact that man can be aware of what is happening to him, can remember, can link occurrences together, can imagine what might occur under other circumstances, and can therefore plan a whole life inclusive of experiences vastly different in their accumulated meaning from any he starts with.

A very simple example will remind us of the differences between human and animal experience. Contrast the very simple diet of animals with that of persons. The human diet like that of the animal has to fit us for survival. Yet who would like to live largely on rice, served in one or two fashions? Perhaps far too many of us are over-impressed by the importance of living by a "human" standard. Rightly or wrongly we insist that food be varied, tasty, served under aesthetic as well as sanitary conditions, eaten in good company. And many of us will make the meal on Thanksgiving Day serve and symbolize high moments in our experience as a nation and as a family. An animal, the most complicated one, hardly can experience such a range of gustatory, social, aesthetic, and religious value in and through the food he eats.

Or, contrast the human experience of fear with that of animals. In human life, fear can expand with every bit of knowledge; it can run the gamut from a simple, almost neutral, startle-response through every shade of anxiety, to dread and horror—and largely because a human being is self-conscious, can remember and can think about what has happened to him and then rebuild his world imaginatively. It is simply disastrous in thinking about persons to forget that the gurgling of a child can become Marian Anderson singing "Sometimes I Feel Like a Motherless Child."

We must remember that in every stage of a man's devel-

opment we are dealing with the developing totality we call
a person. A person is never simply a sum of parts or of the
abilities we distinguished above. He is not simply a collection of abilities and needs. From the beginning, these
activities, as they mature and develop, are connected with
each other in expression and in interaction with the total
environment. A person learns and, as a self-conscious
being, learns from his learnings. This is why a person
learns to give meanings to himself and to others that far
transcend what is possible in an animal. This is why his
body and his bodily capacities can enter into his total experience in so many ways that the meaning of his existence
cannot be spelled out in bodily terms alone. When he is an
infant, he may seem to live for body only, unconsciously or
semi-self-consciously; at the age of 3, similar behavior
would mark him as an idiot.

A person's life, in short, is neither a battle with his body
nor with his supposed bodily appetites; within every dimension of a person there is conflict, and within every
dimension of his life problems need to be solved even as
each dimension is affected by what is going on in the other
dimensions and areas of value. The simple, awesome fact is
that, given the different dimensions of life, a person can
become a Dr. Jekyll and a Mr. Hyde; he can become a Saul
and a St. Paul.

What all this means with regard to sex is that in the best
biomorphic view we misconceive it initially. With a more
personalistic conception of man in view, it is a mistake,
egregious in evil consequences even for sex-education, to
think of sex on a biomorphic model. Sex is not an isolated
physiological force that plows its way unheeding through
all opposition and to which the rest of life must ultimately
be subordinated. We cannot say this even of the more

powerful biological drives of hunger and thirst, for persons do go on hunger strikes for some ideal. Again, it is false to think of persons as pockets of energy that will burst their controls when the time comes; it is false to think of persons as rivers of passion that break down artificial dams. If anything, such models of persons fit people who are sick.

We must not minimize the highly important fact that a person may be dominated by one or another dimension of his being. But we must remember that either domination or subordination can take place only within the initial unity of personal being. A person may be overcome by some desire, but this desire is *his* desire, and as such it is related to other desires that are also his. If this were not so, it would make no sense to say that he comes to control his desires, or to express one desire rather than another.

Convenience in speech will lead us to talk as if "sex" or "emotion" or "intellect" or "will" were separate entities or energies, but the underlying model we must keep in mind is that of a person ranging from the bodily to the religious dimensions of his being. The person in interaction with others develops a "personality." His personality expresses what he has done with the dimensions of his being; it reflects his stage in organizing his value-experiences as he discovers more of what *he* is in relation to others and to his world.

Preadolescent Perspective on Sex and the Person

I shall refuse, then, to talk about a child's sexual development as if it were something separate from his total development. For we must not oversimplifv the complexities of interpreting sex in childhood, as we keep in mind the conclusion of the "Fact-Finding Report to the Mid-Century White House Conference":

> The significance and patterning of sex in child development are incompletely understood and contrastingly interpreted. What is the role of the common childhood experiences in achieving sexual maturity? Psychoanalysis, offering its specific theories of dynamic development, evokes wide disagreement both within its own framework and from without.[4]

Indeed, disagreement often stems from the difference in the underlying view of human nature that investigators bring to the data. The suggestions that follow presuppose the concept of a human being as a person.

The further away we get from the embryonic and infantile state, the less can we treat a child as if he were so much skin wrapped around hunger and other organic needs. Nor is the child a skin wrapped over powerful desires for pleasure springing from the need for oral or anal gratifications—although, once more, to minimize these in a particular situation might well lead to faulty diagnosis. The infant and child experiences desires—for food, exercise and play, physical comfort, and for pleasures connected with the erogenous zones of the body. He cannot, and in any case does not, evaluate the meaning of these desires by himself alone, since he depends so much upon his parents and their evaluation of his actions. What is very important for him, as he grows older, is the kind of regard they hold him in, especially when he does not come up to

[4] Helen L. Witmer and Ruth Kotinsky (eds.), *Personality in the Making* (New York: Harper, 1952), p. 437.

their expectations. An infant needing to suck for food-pleasure may come to suck his thumb, for example. If this becomes a habit and draws the disapproval of his parents, the unhappy child, resenting their disapproval and the displeasure it causes him, may turn secretly to other forms of self-gratification as substitutes without being aware that these too are disapproved. He needs his parents and their approval more than he realizes; but he wants his immediate gratifications too. He does not know why in many instances he cannot have both. He does not understand why his parents, who are usually a source of comfort, now disapprove of such an obvious gratification (value-claim) as, for example, manipulation of his sexual organs. Again, without clearly knowing why, he knows that he needs their approval—even when he wishes he didn't care about it! Uncritical resentment as well as uncritical appreciation build up in him, and all because he depends upon them so much to find out the meaning of his desires and actions.

Sex Education—Not Sex Information

Obviously, I am rejecting any doctrinaire conception of infantile sexuality—or of infantile sin or infantile saintliness for that matter. I am pleading for parents to realize that what John comes to mean to himself depends on how they make themselves felt in his life. The fundamental fact about him, especially in infancy and childhood, is his dependence on them for interpreting his own experiences, that is, the significance of his own actions and of his own value-experience. We thus come back to the importance of the kind of home, the kind of value-system, into which a child is born. Even if John is born into a well-to-do family, he is raised in a psychological slum if his parents have no appreciation of what it means for him, with his own developing potential, to grow up with them (see Chapter 1, pp. 4–8).

If every experience connected with his body is allowed to take its place in the total economy of his growth, without exaggeration and without rigidity of response, John will come to think of himself in relation to his body in a way that allows for further growth. But if mother and father, without being able to explain or even attempting to explain, slap the hand that fondles the penis, is it any wonder that the child may develop ambivalent feelings toward a part of his body as he plays with it when his parents cannot observe? But now he may pay a high price for his pleasure in anxiety at the thought of their disapproval or of some punishment that may somehow be visited upon him. The informed and patient (how easy to *say* this!) parent must devise ways of correcting the child wisely and affectionately.

What our varied sources of evidence forcibly suggest, in the midst of much obscurity, is that it is important for the growing child to know that he can make "mistakes" without being excluded from the basic concern and care of his parents. Sentimental or "permissive" love alone will never take the place of understanding and insight into John's problem of self-discovery, but the assurance that his parents will not leave him "in the cold" to fend for himself is crucial to John's own willingness to try again. The most comfortable physical surroundings will never take the place of a home—an atmosphere in which the growing child can feel that he is important for himself, that mistakes will not be considered irrevocable as he does his best to "be good."

It is within this context that we must understand the aim of sex *education*. Providing sex *information* is not enough. If behavior involving the sexual organs can be interpreted so that the child will develop emotionally "clean" attitudes toward them and if sex-related questions can be welcomed and answered with a view to keeping information linked with interest and insight into other facts about life, the child will have made a good beginning. But if he finds negative attitudes or an eloquent silence toward sex questions, he is left free to imagine all sorts of things and to explore himself in secret, his self-knowledge being at the mercy of scraps of information picked up from others equally blind.

What is worse, such eloquent silence actually can create a psychological rift between parent and child on a topic that is important to the child. In the course of any day the normal youngster will have plenty of provocation to explore himself and others; sex information need not be expected to decrease such enticements. But self-exploration and the exploration of others may gain even greater prestige and power over him because he is dealing with an area of disturbance for him rather than with experiences that can be kept in the area of normal interest and communication. Here an interested casualness would seem the best atmosphere for the parent to try to create. If the youngster can come to pubescence with fairly clear ideas about the meaning of sexual abilities, the changes brought by adolescence will come as more of a transition than a crisis.

Yet it was a 19-year-old college junior, the daughter of college graduates, who came with great anxiety to talk about the time her male cousin and she, at the age of 10, had tried to have sexual intercourse. She could not tell her parents, she said, but all these years she worried about her

own feeling of guilt and disappointment in herself. Her
well-appointed house was not a home. Her attractive personality was struggling with doubts about the meaning of
her sexuality.

The sexual dimension of personal life, let me repeat,
must be evaluated both in terms of its own characteristic
value and in terms of its relation to other dimensions of
personal experience. In the preadolescent period, what sex
comes to mean to a boy or girl will depend in good measure on his or her sense of it as normal and not peculiarly
distinctive. Unfortunate traumatic experiences aside, sexuality need present no special problems. The preadolescent has been evaluating his experiences with himself and
others within the range of values dominating his home life
and his community. During the years from 4 to 6, he had
already begun to be less absorbed with himself and to lay
the foundation for the new sense of self that grows apace
between 6 and 12. As Gordon W. Allport aptly describes
these years:

> The child's sense of identity, his self-image, and his
> capacity for self-extension are greatly enhanced by his
> entrance into school. His classmates are frank and
> brutal regarding his weaknesses and idiosyncracies ...
> but they also help establish an identity and render
> more acute the inner sense of selfhood.
>
> The child soon learns that what is expected of him
> outside the home is very different from parental
> standards. A boy must soon learn to shift rapidly from
> the harsh and obscene talk of his peers to the politer
> world of his parents, and somehow to incorporate
> both worlds into his own being. When the children
> enter their peer society they have a sharp lesson in

"reality testing." They learn in effect to say, "Now I must do this. Now I must do that. Now I must be careful. Now I can do what I please." Such shifts intensify the sense of self.

It is well known that children of this age become moralistic and legalistic. Rules of the game must be followed rigidly. Parental rules are important, but the rules of the gang are utterly binding. The child does not yet trust himself to be an independent moral agent. His sense of self is comfortable only if he adapts to outer rules, extends himself to his gang, and develops a self-image of a safe conformer. The child fiercely believes that his family, his religion, and also his peer-group are right. While he may feel conflict between parent and peer standards, he is firmly loyal to these particular extensions of himself.

All the while the child's intellectual life is developing . . . Objective knowledge fascinates him, and the question "Why?" is always on his lips. He begins to sense a new power, a new aspect of his selfhood.[5]

In short, the closer the child comes to adolescence, the more he is caught in evaluating, in thinking about his own value-experiences and those he has accepted from others. Adolescence, though we need not think of it as a precipitous break with the past, adds a new ferment in the life of the youngster. One might almost say that changes in bodily development are symbolic of the other changes. The girl undergoing changes does not know whether she will continue to be "so pretty"; one 15-year-old boy, distressed by

[5] Gordon W. Allport, *Pattern and Growth in Personality*, pp. 123-124. Copyright 1937, © 1961 by Holt, Rinehart and Winston, Inc. Reprinted by permission of Holt, Rinehart and Winston, Inc.

the fact that he was shorter than most boys his age, asked his father anxiously: "Do you think I'll grow another inch at least?"

Ferment and change, then, all the way from physical identity to total self-identity become the rule. The adolescent is aware that new formations, some quite discontinuous with the old, are taking place. As Erik H. Erikson has emphasized, the questions become increasingly: Who am I? Where do I stand in relation to others? What is the point of what I'm doing? Can *I* live up to what is expected of me? What can I really do? What can I depend upon others to do? Can it be that the God I have heard about does exist and cares? What ought I to do with my life?[6]

When John left home for kindergarten or the first grade, he was still quite dependent upon his parents, for whom his schoolteachers were little more than substitutes. But when John has lived 12 or 15 years, together with his added emotional and intellectual powers, he is caught in a new childhood that is not childhood. He still needs his parents—more than he cares to admit—and yet he does not want to be treated like a child. At the same time he may hate to have more expected of him by his parents and his society than he thinks he may be able to deliver. Somehow these parents—themselves caught between being pals and judges—seem to him not to understand. "It's easy for them to talk and preach, but I'm the one that's got to live with them and with myself and the gang. They just don't seem to know the score. Can anyone understand me—including myself? Nobody knows the trouble I have!" The adolescent involved in accelerated change is in search of what his

[6] See especially E. H. Erikson, *The Child and Society* (2d rev. ed.; New York: Norton, 1964).

existence can mean. He would like to find someone to help him understand it—and bear it!

It is to this kind of ferment in the rest of his life that sexual growth adds new emotional responses toward self and toward members of the opposite sex. Boy or girl already accepts the idea that marriage and family are as much a part of future existence as finding a job. But with the onset of new sexual emotion, the meaning of marriage and family is realized, and with an undreamed of significance! Under the power of the sexual emotion that makes one so sensitive and excitingly responsive to the looks and touch of the opposite sex, the adolescent can find himself literally magnetized by another 15-year-old of the other sex who seems to understand, to be a "real pal." The push of his own inner excitement in response to the pull of her attractiveness and the images she conjures up in dreams and daydreams—this is a new situation.

But, as we have insisted, since the adolescent is a person and not an animal, he will cope with this situation in relation to the totality of what he knows, feels, imagines, and can do up to that point. Here, of course, he must draw upon his total relation to his home and his past, and his earlier sex education becomes one of his resources. The situation, however, becomes so complex that it must be described in some detail.

Sex in the Search for Meaning

Our youngster comes to pubescence, let us assume for our purposes here, without special feelings of anxiety and with a basic understanding of biological changes and capacities. Part of the adolescent ferment will involve his own appreciation of a sexual emotion for which we might use the word *lust,* had this word not been spoiled by unfortunate negative connotations. The important fact is that this new emotion, accompanying the maturation of sexual organs and functions, brings its own psychic focus and power into the adolescent's life.

As with other emotions like fear, anger, sympathy, or elation, the sexual emotion prepares the whole person for action. When we experience sexual emotion, our total being is stirred and predisposed in thought and action to explore and possess the person that is the sexual object for us.[7] There is nothing unclean or morally wrong about this exciting and inciting emotion as such; the adolescent's earlier experience and education should, at best, predispose him to this view. But the person who comes into adolescence with anxiety or guilt feelings about his sexuality is likely to extend these feelings to the sexual emotion. To "accept it" does not mean to regard his sexuality as a mischievous troublemaker, but to realize that he can deal with it effectively once he stops thinking of himself as a "poor victim," as a "little animal," and stops seeking once-and-for-all solutions. With a kind of good humor he can learn to say to himself: Sex has been around for a long time, and every human being has had to learn what part it could play in his life. My turn has come, and I have already learned that self-pity doesn't help and that I can control powerful emotions, especially after I have been honest with them. I may find I'm not as strong as I

[7] Normally this would be a member of the opposite sex, but I am purposely not using that expression because the same would be true in homosexual relationships.

thought, but I may lose a few battles without losing the war. Certainly, many other human beings I know seem to have done so.

All this is, of course, easier for the grown-up moralist to say than for the adolescent to do; yet, let us face the situation realistically. No adolescent grows up just by letting things take their course, or merely by "talking about things." He, too, wittingly or unwittingly, makes up his mind about himself and what line he is going to take with himself. His elders can help him to see what the directions are. As regards sex, for example, what is involved is a basic attitude toward his sexuality. He can think of this as a discharge of emotion—and he will be correct up to a point. Whether it is only a discharge for the rest of his life is the problem he cannot escape. It involves the whole meaning of his character and creativity.

The problem is: Can I transform this *discharge* into an *expression* of what life means to me? He already knows this problem with regard to all the other emotional "discharges" in his life—such as anger, fear, elation, respect, sympathy, tenderness, greed. When he does not ask what he wants a given emotion to be, in his own life and in relation to others, the emotion is never *expressed;* it merely discharges in him! For an adolescent to discover himself, for him to participate in the meaning his own life will have, is for him to begin right where he is in this life-long encounter with the meaning his emotions are to take.

Discharge or expression? It is this underlying problem that concerns us in the remainder of this book. Since I am not concerned here with the discussion of homosexual emotion and behavior, I shall confine myself to the prob-

lems of emotional attachment as they take form in relation
to members of the opposite sex and, to begin with, in relation to petting.

Petting and the Sexual Progression[8]

Since the sexual emotion is new and its gratification
gives pleasure, it encourages the pleasure-giving exploration called *petting*. This should not surprise us, though we
should remember that the experience involves wonder and
curiosity about oneself as well as about the other person.
But other emotions are also involved—more than we can
distinguish. To regard petting as mainly a lustful response
is to underestimate the different important ways in which
young people enter each other's lives. Is it strange that two
young people who like each other, who enjoy talking together, being together, and playing together should want
to caress each other as another way of showing and finding
approval for each other? Aesthetic and social sensitivity are
seldom absent from heterosexual relationships. The sexual
emotion may be the initiating factor in petting, but petting must be understood as part of the total meaning a
particular person assigns to himself in relation to members
of the opposite sex.

Why then make a moral issue out of petting? The answer is that initially there is no more and no less a moral
issue here than there is about any other experienced value-
claim. A person's moral problem is always that of choosing
a pattern of value-claims that will not endanger other
value-claims. Every youth needs to consider and choose

[8] This theme has been elaborated in the author's *The Human Venture
in Sex, Love, and Marriage* (New York: Association Press, 1949), Chapter 1.

what part he wants his sexuality to play in relation to the rest of his values, including the values of members of the opposite sex to him. Hence, what is at issue is more than sex-value in petting; it is the way in which petting enters into his relation to others. With regard to petting, the danger lies in taking it either too seriously or not seriously enough. Yet, because the basic considerations for evaluating petting are not unlike those involved in more intimate relationships between man and woman, it will repay us to analyze them with some care.

First, because petting is so pleasant and seems so innocent, John and his new-found partner, Jane, may underestimate the power of their own emotions as they respond to each other's touch. They soon find themselves moving from hands and lips to caressing and fondling their bodies simply because this is what it means to be sexually aroused and responsive. Psychologically, petting, linked with tender endearments, consists of the mutual stimulation that prepares the person and the sexual organs physiologically for sexual intercourse and its climax in orgasm. Both John and Jane need to be aware that the caressing of Jane's breasts and body, and the stimulation of the vagina and the clitoris, produce a total state of excitement that makes sexual intercourse itself the increasingly desired, if not inevitable, end. What began simply as fondling can set up a chain reaction that is neither expected nor approved, yet is all but uncontrollable.

Many adolescents engage in light petting with no thought of intercourse and, too much privacy aiding, find themselves carried beyond limits. They have not counted on other factors driving toward further petting and, finally, copulation. To be wanted by another, to feel one's control over another, to feel sympathy and tenderness toward another in need, to be fascinated by another's, as well as one's own, response—these and many other emotions can come flooding into the total experience. Is it any wonder that their desires, now felt to be elevating as well as powerful, take them "out of this world" in excitement and release?

Second, John and Jane will need to keep in mind *sexual progression*. Let us assume that Jane and John began holding hands. When they first found that they liked each other, holding hands symbolized the wonderful new link between them. The progression begins when they find that holding hands is mere preparation for kissing and embracing. Kissing and embracing soon give way to further caressing, and so on. Yet they find that each successive step of the progression, needed to bring sexual release or *gratification*, brings no more *satisfaction* than the earlier stage. Each new step is meaningful and gratifying to begin with; each involves "discharge of tension" and seems to express their wanting at that stage. But this stage soon ceases in itself to gratify, and it leaves them with a longing for another step. If John and Jane should stop going together, they may find that with other partners they skip the earlier, "boring" steps in the sexual progress, for they are likely to be driven by a different level of wanting.

What happens in the sexual progression, then, is that the point for gratification tends to move on without materially increasing the *quality* of the gratification. John and Jane may feel a "relief" that itself sets the point of gratification "next time," so the relief can intensify the tension they were trying to release. Sex desire is like an arrow pointed toward a target—it is easier to release it, to allow it to "discharge," then to control its acceleration. Suppose that John and Jane are carried to a more intimate mutual stimulation and then to sexual intercourse. Will the new demand for release through sexual intercourse satisfy them and link them together as persons? Or will John and Jane, having developed no other adequate links to bind them than immediate gratification, find that even their mutual gratification seems to decrease in value? Just as they had quickly lost interest in the earlier stages of petting, will they rapidly come to the end of gratification in each other? Will there be a disappointment even in their emotional discharge because its gratification did not keep in step with their total development? And will they then begin again the search for a new source of gratification also unrelated to the full demands of their growth?

I certainly cannot assert with absolute certainty that this will happen, but what good reason, in a specific instance, is there for supposing that these changes will not take place? John and Jane certainly cannot assume that what has happened to so many others will not happen to them. They thought they were "so good for each other," but now they begin to feel trapped by the escalation of their own desires —which seem to want gratification for their own sake, no matter who the partner is. It is an old story: John leaves Jane for Janet, and then flits to Jeanne, seeking greater variety, greater novelty. But is he satisfied as a person?

It is easy for the adolescent to be seduced into thinking that the "expression" of sex alone will solve his problem. Actually, he may be trying to put out a fire by throwing gasoline on it! There is more "discharge," or relief of tension, than satisfying expression.

Sex—for Fun?

Petting, then, may not only open the floodgates to emotions of unsuspected violence but also may lead to an escalation of desire that increases the grip of habit without affording increase in quality. John and Jane will do well, before they encourage a chain of emotional discharge and reaction, to take a second look at sex and petting "for fun." For the question comes down to this. Can the sexual emotion be discharged in isolation without setting up a self-absorbing demand for its own gratification? Will petting-for-fun, will "sex for release" cause more emotional problems in each life than are solved?

Sex-pleasure has its own quality, or, better, its own kind of quality, and builds up power as a habit of achieving pleasure. Even assuming that it could be isolated from his other needs, a person is still faced with the formidable task of discovering how to control the tempo, or momentum, and expression of his sexual desire. Otherwise, its unharnessed power could subordinate every other value to what could become an orgiastic ritual that cruelly victimizes him when he is in fact seeking relief.

Nevertheless, the sexual emotion, like any other primary emotion, is not evil in itself; it comes into an adolescent life with exciting promise. It is because sex experience can contribute its own kind of quality of life—apart from any procreative biological function—that the adolescent must learn to manage his sexual emotion so that it can contribute its value to his life without endangering other values. For sex comes with its emotional power into a life that is coping with other problems. To the extent that the adolescent fails in his relationships to those who help to frame the meanings of his own adventures, falls short of achieving the respect of his peers—thus finding life disappointing and dull—to this extent he may be thrown back upon the pleasures that he carries about in his own psychophysiological being.

Thus, the masturbation, or self-petting, that might well have been an occasional, tension-reducing source of sex-pleasure with no serious emotional or physiological consequences can now become a frequent and continuous source of gratification that is expected to make up for other disappointments. Yet, again, masturbation can create more problems than it solves as a source of sexual relief. For it becomes a means of escaping from other frustrations by producing self-absorbed and introverted habits of sexual response. These habits of response do not augur well for a relationship to be established some day with another person whose tempo and responsiveness are different.

Accordingly, as with petting generally, the consequences of masturbation are not to be seen merely in biomorphic terms,[9] but in light of the part masturbation plays in the total economy of sexual discovery and self-confidence. In this larger relationship the evil of self-manipulation lies not only in inducing sexual relief that may be more difficult to obtain as time passes, but also in a habit of finding release for tensions that concentrate on self-responsiveness rather than on sensitivity to the responsiveness of another. The person who wants to use his sexuality to love another, to meet the needs of his partner-in-love, can know deep frustration and disappointment because he is caught in the coils of his own sexual tempo and self-absorbed focus. Be-

[9] See Richard F. Hettlinger, *Living with Sex: The Student's Dilemma* (New York: The Seabury Press, 1966) for a good treatment of this problem and for an excellent evaluation of "the Playboy philosophy" as well as other problems we have been discussing.

cause masturbation itself can be the seductive and unproductive refuge of a bitterly disappointed person, it can, especially in the life of an immature adult, gain a grip it does not deserve; it can injure his self-esteem so badly that he loses confidence in his capacity to be successful in his sexual (and total) relationship to a member of the opposite sex.

Sex—With Affection?

Finally, since petting is normally turned outward toward a member of the opposite sex, the role it plays here must also be analyzed, and once more in terms of its value in the growth of a person. It may be that John is using Jane, or Jane is using John, simply as a means of getting an easy pleasure; they may become, by mutual if largely implicit agreement, playthings for each other. Or John may be using Jane (or vice versa) in a way that would be resented when recognized, as a means of proving his sexual prowess; she is merely another conquest.

A human relationship is never richer than what two persons bring to it. Petting pleasure by itself can keep them going together for a while. But younger adolescents in particular may not be aware that they are using petting as a means of compensating for other disappointments, since petting in itself gives them experience in knowing what their sexual responsiveness is. Once petting has become normal between them, it can be much more difficult for them to explore the other ways in which two human beings can be interesting to each other. Hence, the adolescent has to face as part of his "petting problem" the issues that his parents and his society have to solve in industrial and political relationships: Ought I to exploit other persons for my own gratification even if they don't mind? Two people who have very little in common can always "have a drink" or eat together. A couple who really have nothing to say to each other, who share no other dimensions of value, still have their bodies as a common denominator, so they can always turn to petting as a way out of what would otherwise be an idle and boring relationship.

Is this much ado about nothing? I can hear a critic exclaim: "Aren't you making mountains out of molehills? Aren't you going out of your way to look for trouble? Why can't two adolescents just have some sexual pleasures with affection without our being kill-joys? Why not let it be a way of making up for other tensions or for feeling even momentarily important?"

Let me first reply that I am considering what it means to talk about sex education and pleading that we get beyond physiological facts to the values in human development. But, second, I wish that the answers to his questions were as obvious as my critic seems to think. I suggest that anyone who ceases to think of sex as an independent physiological mechanism, who becomes aware of the many facets involved in sexual experimentation, must think twice. Indeed, he may come to recognize that the caution recommended in matters of sex in the Judeo-Christian tradition[10] is founded on a deeper sense of the psychic forces in persons than it is sometimes given credit for.

Therefore, I must decry a certain sentimental naïveté

[10] See William Graham Cole, *Sex and Love in the Bible* (New York: Association Press, 1959), as well as his *Sex in Christianity and Psychoanalysis* (New York: Oxford University Press, 1955); see also William P. Wylie, *Human Nature and Christian Marriage* (London: Student Christian Movement Press, 1958).

about the situations we allow our young people to get into without adequate counseling that involves this choice of value. Therefore, my main preliminary concern is to keep the total development of the person before us lest we be too easily seduced into thinking that even the sexual experimentation that is involved in petting can be dissociated from the larger value-choices an adolescent can make.

My basic concern is to keep sexuality itself meaningful and constructive in the life of a person. Dr. Mary Calderone has put it neatly: "No one knows what effect sex, precociously experienced, will have on the immature psyche."[11] Sexual experimentation can create larger problems than it solves, especially if it is narrowly self-absorbed or if it is basically exploitive of another. The "little kiss," the "skin you love to touch"—we hear such "harmless" slogans for such "playful" acts as if it were a case of dogs casually rubbing noses.

Yet, as a matter of fact, a human kiss can and does mean many things. And John and Jane must decide what meanings they shall use it to express. Shall it be saved for those occasions when, in addition to offering sex-pleasure and aesthetic pleasure, it *also* becomes a way of expressing gratitude or appreciation of the link they both feel? Shall it be connected with moments of impersonal desire when anyone of the opposite sex could be its object? Shall it be used to say a "hello" one does not mean or a "good-bye" one does not regret? As one college freshman put it: "She kissed me good night, and I could just hear: 'Thank God you're going!' "

The language of feeling, like the language of poetry, need not be effete but must always preserve and improve

[11] "The Case for Chastity," in *Sex in America*, ed. H. A. Grunwald (New York: Bantam Books, 1964), p. 143.

the capacity to mean. Let John and Jane decide what their petting is about and then what really gives it meaning. They do not have to be prudes; but they must establish, as it were, the grammar and syntax of their relationship. If the kiss expresses the friendship and companionship they enjoy on many other counts, their answer to the question of meaning will be different than if their petting is their main source of enjoyment. Each must then face the fact that their temptation will be to explore more intimate and exciting ways of gratifying each other. Are they willing to go "all the way" before that consummation can be emotionally and imaginatively reinforced by social commitment and religious symbol? Do they realize that to "go all the way" under other auspices increases the chances, inherent in the sexual progression when left to itself, to want to go "all the way" with a new lover? On the other hand, if they like each other and enjoy each other, will they not want to save their best for the best occasion and thus avoid becoming emotional problems for each other sexually?

Perhaps the following story will illustrate some of the complexities we have been considering. A mother I know had answered her daughter Mary's questions about sex very intelligently as she grew older, and Mary at 16 was not unaware of the sexual progression. Yet a crisis arose. I shall report first the mother's point of view: "Mary, as girls her age are wont to do these days, has been going with Andy for about two years, as her steady. Andy, who is seventeen and a half, is by no means irresponsible, and he is well thought of at school by his teachers and his classmates; he expects to go to college.

"I know Mary. She not only has the kind of body attractive to men, but she is a warm, outgoing personality, and I would be silly not to suppose that they are not petting.

Unfortunately, I am living in a community where parents are permissive because they just don't know what to do with these strong and healthy young people. Well, frankly, I'm concerned about Mary's possible involvement in the later stages of what you call the sexual progression. My husband leaves the whole thing in my hands, but expects me to see that Mary doesn't get into trouble. Mary is now touchy about my questions, and tells me, angrily and bitterly, that I don't trust her. Sometimes I'm driven to distraction by my fears, and I have surprised myself at my willingness even to open Mary's correspondence."

As we chatted about the matter, I asked whether she wanted Mary to reach, say, the age of 25 without knowing what it meant to be sexually aroused or what her strong emotions could tempt her to do. The mother, reflecting on her own experience, replied with a hesitant *"no."* We realized that some decisions would have to be left to Mary herself, once everything was done to make her feel that she was trusted and that her parents did care about her whole future. But the mother prevailed upon me as a friend to chat with Mary if she would come.

When Mary came to talk, it soon became evident that she was as much aware of the possible dangers as her mother. In substance, she said: "I know that mother is concerned about me, and while I do get angry with her snooping, I must confess that Andy and I have had our troubles. It is easy to be alone these days, what with cars and unchaperoned parties. I like Andy and we've been good for each other. But pretty soon I realized that caressing beyond kissing could arouse me plenty and make it much harder for him to control himself. We began to dread this part of our being together. We finally talked it out.

"Andy is going to college and has four years in which he

will probably change a great deal. In another year I'm hoping to go to college. A lot of water can go under the bridge. We realized that we didn't want to get each other used to more than we could accept responsibility for. So we decided where we would stop and to help each other keep within that safe distance. Of course, it's not easy, but it makes a lot of difference to know that we both know what the score is and can go on being friends. I think now that Andy will not be hurt by me and that another girl, if that's what it comes to, will get a very nice guy. And, if it's not Andy, in about five years I hope another man is going to get a girl that Andy did not use just for fun. Andy and I have helped each other to grow up, and I've got no regrets. At least Andy cannot say that I encourage him to take on more than he would approve in his calmer moments. I don't blame Mother for being worried, but see if you cannot get her to relax more about this."

Mary and Andy had reached the point, in other words, where they found that sex-values were endangering other values, present and future, in their experience. Without being censorious or sentimental, without self-pity or self-righteousness, they were trying to keep their petting experiences within the larger pattern of values they approved for their future lives as they could foresee them. In their lives other emotional and intellectual needs were converging with and challenging the sexual sensitivity that was so immediate and strong, and they realized that their petting problem was part of their total self-knowledge and growth.

They and their parents could have played all the angles safely by ensuring that an unwanted pregnancy would not occur if they went "too far." Perhaps they could have their cake of immediate gratification and eat it too, that is, keep the quality of sex growing. But neither they nor their parents could increase the meaning of sex in their lives by keeping them biologically safe. Sex could easily have become an experience meaning failure in self-control and failure in mutual appreciation and helpfulness. As it was, this couple had learned to make it play an important, but limited, part in their friendship.[12]

The above discussion may make it clear why so many young people and their parents have frequently felt that my stand on petting is wishy-washy. They have wanted me to say "yes" or "no." And my answer is that in this total premarital development the person needs to realize that his sexual habits and his attitudes toward himself as a person, to members of the other sex as persons, are the foundation for attitudes and habits of later life. How can he keep fun from becoming exploitation, and how can he keep affection from becoming conquest as he learns to live with persons of the opposite sex? He will have to determine "policy" in terms of his decision to "use" or "not to use" persons for his own pleasure. He will then ask: "How far can I go as a friend in a *mutual* friendship?"

Having said all this, suppose Andy and Mary were 20, closer to the time of marriage, and in love? Would there be any good reason for their not welcoming the sexual progression as part of their love? To this question we must now turn.

---

[12] See the well-balanced article "Sex or Guilt," by the psychiatrist at Vassar College, Robert E. Nixon, in *Sex in America*, ed. H. A. Grunwald (New York: Bantam Books, 1964), pp. 126-140.

5 *DO SEX AND LOVE NEED MARRIAGE?*

The question before us throughout this book has been: How can the quality of the sexual experience be protected? What habits of thought, of emotion, of behavior are likely to keep sex from making a continued, creative difference in the life of a person? These questions cannot be answered intelligently without tracing the relation of sexual values to other values, without considering how one set of experiences and values opens the way for, and encourages the growth of, other sets of experiences and values. Because we are persons, because we are "fighters for values," and because values are connected with one another, we cannot isolate one part of our lives from the rest of our being. Every person always faces the practical problem of figuring out relations between values and disvalues stemming from any course of action. And we have seen that a victim of the sexual progression loses confidence in his ability to control his sexual desires; in so doing he decreases, restricts, and may even destroy the possibility of other values equally important to him as a human being. But will this approach be relevant to questions that keep on coming up with renewed insistence from younger and older persons alike? Let us see.

Is Sex for "Frank" Mutual Fun Enough?

Suppose that a couple asks: "If we protect ourselves against venereal disease and pregnancy, if we don't take ourselves too seriously and decide to express our liking for each other in sexual intercourse until our mutual attraction ceases, what harm do we do?

In the light of what we have already said, we may pose in return four questions: Do you think that you can trust yourselves to each other's sexual responses in this relatively casual way without affecting yourselves in other ways? Do you think that you can treat sex merely as a kind of good-natured fun with a convenient partner at one time and then also use it as a way of communicating other meanings at another time with the person you love? How do you plan to escape the mentality of the philanderer who, in his "fun," is increasingly the victim of his desire for a new conquest? How do you escape from becoming increasingly unscrupulous in your relation toward your sex partner?

These questions are meant to be more than rhetorical. For to speak of sex just for "red-blooded" fun seems so "natural" and "youthful." But does the "artistic lover" really overcome his desire to "win his subject over"? Does the adjective "red-blooded" not mean that he has the unquestioned "right" to use his prowess over those who cannot resist his charms? Does "sex for the single girl" or "for the single man" actually free persons from inhibitions, or do they become inhibited in their freedom as persons? The person who sets out on this course should at least be honest with himself and realize that at best he is saying: "I do not want sex-fun to involve me in the value-experience of others any more than a casual discussion or a game of tennis would."

Again, this may seem theoretically a fair and reasonable attitude, especially when the two "adult" principals are fully agreed. In practice, the complexity of the human being, the fact that sex cannot be isolated from the total personality, makes such a situation unreal. One person "loves" in a different way from another and does so unsuspectingly. Jane, for example, may convince herself that she is willing to enter into a frank and open "fun" or "release" relationship with John that will be terminated at the wish of either with "no recriminations and no regrets." But can she control the rhythm of desire? Can she restrict the intensity, the depth, and the outreach of what may have come to mean more to her "poise" than she realized? When John is ready to "call it off," does Jane, enmeshed in coils she did not dream could be so strong, simply move to another lover with no hurt because she is not pregnant?

Nor can we be satisfied with the reply: "John has the moral right, because of their previous explicit agreement, to think only of his own convenience. It's not his 'problem' but Jane's!" Sex would have to be a mere external mechanism that can be shut off and on in the life of a person for this answer to go unquestioned. But sex is not that kind of mechanism in a person, and if it becomes that, the person has already been badly hurt. What in our whole human experience would make us think that John can go unscathed through a series of such experiences, hardening himself against caring for his partner because they had agreed theoretically that no such concern should be required? And is he a better person because, for the same reason, he has learned to harden himself, when he is left behind, against any feeling of betrayal and abandonment?

Is this, then, what "mature gaiety for mature people"

comes to? One cannot avoid the feeling that a "fun" philosophy of sex is one of the symptoms of an age too much
given to mechanisms. Such a "sex-is-fun" philosophy,
sounding so deceptively "human," is actually neither
humane nor humanistic nor humanitarian. If this is what
it means to have "sex without guilt," one may well wonder
whether a new source of guilt had better not develop to
keep John alive to the fact that he is reducing himself to
treating other persons like cars—for "joy rides" only!

Apart from a certain moral callousness lying below the
superficial sophistication of the "fun" philosophy, there
are other, perhaps more tangible, disadvantages that John
will have to consider. One is the diminishing returns "fun-
wise," as habit tends to level off the novelty. He will join
in the increasingly frantic search by the fun-lovers for convenient partners who, in proportion to their sophistication, have also learned to concentrate on the "thrill" but
not on the person.

But perhaps we are pushing John too far toward the
excess where even "fun" ceases to be "fun" and becomes
addiction. He may be thinking of a little "fun" before marriage, even as a preparation for marriage. The question
here is whether his attitude toward sexuality, determining
habit and determined by habit, is a promising preparation
for his ideal of sex in marriage. Does he think it will be a
simple matter to shift from an attitude toward sexual intercourse that amounts to little more than a demand for
mutual masturbation to one of willing adjustment to the
needs of another that marriage requires? Or will he be
forced psychologically to treat his wife as he had his mis-
tresses?

If human experience teaches us anything, it tells us that

the hardest shifts we make are those from self-absorption, from using others, to entering into patient and trusting concern for them. Hence my answer to persons who talk about sex for fun, or sex without guilt, is that they could find no easier way to run sexual values to the ground and to encourage a casualness about human relations that is basically at variance with our stronger desire to be cared for and to care. Human beings cannot be turned into soft-drink vending machines set up for "refreshment" or a "lift," where one dime does the job as well as another, or one bottle is like another. To treat each other for amusement only is to sow the wind of self-absorption and eventually to reap the whirlwind of lonely isolation. Human beings can "protect" themselves against venereal disease and pregnancy; they can use pills to avoid physical disaster —but when they do they are dying as persons.

We are now ready to formulate the conclusion forced upon us which we need to test further in the light of an even more important question: *Sexuality decreases in the contribution it makes to a given life to the extent that it is isolated from other needs, abilities, and ventures in value; it increases in value to the extent that it becomes a way of expressing other needs as well, to the extent that it symbolizes other values that draw persons together as persons.* To the degree that sexual emotion can become a positive theme in the symphony of values and expressive of a larger vocation (in the sense defined above, pp. 52–54), it grows in meaning and value. The bodily link expresses the unity the two persons feel as they grow together.

Is Sexual Anxiety a Product of
Unnecessary Social Pressure?

The whole thesis I have been exploring has been challenged over and over again by persons who have felt that it
does not take adequate account of the fact that a person's
"sexual conscience" is formed by the unfortunate pressures
of social training, especially in his early years. This point
of view is well-expressed by a 25-year-old graduate student
in the social sciences who, having read the manuscript this
far, wrote: "I think you are fundamentally correct in your
analysis of the 'sex is fun' thesis, and I think it should give
pause to those who take for granted what may be called the
'Playboy philosophy.' But I keep on wondering about
what I now ask you.

"Briefly, I think I grant that *most* people in *our* society
cannot take such casual liaisons casually. People I have
known who have been involved in 'affairs' of one sort or
another seem to have emerged emotionally crippled in one
way or another. I've often thought that if I became involved with a girl who, for one reason or another, craved a
high degree of sexual involvement as a reassuring aspect of
the relationship—a not too unpleasant thought at first
glance!—I would ultimately have to beware of the casualness of the relationship on the grounds that such a person
in our culture is in fact quite likely to emerge from a
'casual' affair very much scarred emotionally.

"In other words, isn't the danger and the naïveté of the
'sex-is-fun' philosophy caused by the fact that it is being
purveyed in a culture in which traditional sexual norms
are such that even now defiance of them is potentially
catastrophic for the individual? Because our culture has

not treated sex casually, those who advocate that people be allowed to treat it casually now are advocating a dysfunction that many Americans, at least, cannot stand.

"However, it may be that in my children's generation the casual affair may be a possibility without serious psychological anxiety. I can conceive of a society in which sex is conceived of differently and does not in fact cause the personal value-disruptions we now face so often in America. Needless to point out, we do know societies where casual sex is in fact a norm—the bonds of marriage being formed in other ways—and produces none of the conflicts of an intense personal psychological sort that casual sex in our society so often produces. But I'm wondering whether, right as you essentially are about the 'sex-is-fun' philosophy in our society, you will not be wrong when a different cultural evaluation of sex is accepted."

Other critics may phrase this point differently. It lies at the core of some of the resentment that young people feel. For, confronted by the strength of their sexual desires and by the inner control exercised by their sexual training, they feel trapped by what they tend to consider, after all, as only the arbitrary demands of their culture. If only they lived in another culture, they could do "what comes naturally" without anxiety.

One cannot deal with this argument briefly without seeming dogmatic. But when it is linked with the biomorphic view of sex and man (see above, pp. 73–77), it forms much of the foundation of the philosophy of those who believe that we ought to create a new cultural norm concerning sex. The issues would take us into difficult problems about the nature of man and his relation to social norms.

All I can do here[1] is first to insist that very important issues *are* involved and then to ask the reader to realize that from the beginning of this book I have been asking: "What *ought* we to become as persons?" Far from denying that we are influenced by our culture, I have been asking: "What kind of person do we wish our culture to produce, or, what do we mean by a good culture?" To be sure, other cultures are surviving; so are many persons walking the streets! The question is: How can survival bring out the best in human nature? The ideal for the person, the symphony of values, is suggested as a minimal core of what keeps persons creative.

I should want to defend this pattern of values as one to which all persons, everywhere, should aspire *as soon as possible* in their growth as persons. I have already urged that even in the individual life we cannot impose a value-pattern like a mold upon a person at a given stage of development. But just as the specific orchestration, or working out, of a value-pattern needs to take account of individual differences, so will different cultures need to work toward a symphony of values in the light of all the factors that would be involved in the social realization of value.

Yet many social scientists are themselves warning us that it is dangerous to compare one phenomenon in a culture (in this case, for example, the expression of sex and the forms of marriage and family) with a similar one in another culture without realizing the ramifications of that phenomenon on others. What a society seems to gain at one point involves serious losses at others. The art of choosing in an individual life is paralleled by the art of

[1] But see Peter A. Bertocci and Richard M. Millard, *Personality and the Good* (New York: McKay, 1963), Chapters 7, 8, 9, 13, 14, 15 for an extended discussion of the relativity of values.

working toward the best possible in social and political life. But in both instances choosing will become sheer opportunism unless guided by a critical policy that is aware of the difficulty in achieving desirable value-growth in the lives of persons. I shall return to this question in the final chapter of this book.

At any rate, the issue we must face today in *our* culture is whether, on the basis of what we know, it will be better, less guilt-producing or anxiety-increasing, for persons to engage in casual sex. And here, considerations of the sort advanced in this book cannot be disregarded. The underlying question for any culture, as for any person, is: In what areas of life do we want to increase anxieties because we do wish to attain certain ideals? If, for example, we do want children to be born in *homes* and in the kind of community in which persons do feel linked to each other in as many value-enterprises as possible, why should we be unwilling to create the conditions for persons' feeling both anxiety and guilt if they do not meet sexual norms? What a person can feel anxious about, what he feels guilty about, may well be a measure of his own growth, of his own relations to others, and of his own level of social responsibility. To say that we ought to relax sexual standards because many people feel too anxious or guilty when they break them is like saying that we ought to change standards about theft or about civil rights for similar reasons.

What I am suggesting here must not be misunderstood. We must never relax in the task of having persons understand why they should behave as they are expected to behave. For this reason I have been urging more thorough sex education, not mere sex information, in this book. But part of that education includes discussion of this issue among others. I am asking whether it is not naïve to sup-

pose that we can have the good that we do have in any
society without creating anxiety? Perhaps the question is
never: Can I avoid anxiety? but, rather, What anxiety is
needless? What anxiety is inevitable? What anxiety is
worth accepting as creatively as possible? Our problem as
persons and citizens is to face the conflicts in our lives
honestly and to accept our responsibility of living with,
and not off, each other parasitically. Neither we nor our
children can live with each other as if the aim of life is to
avoid anxiety, or even guilt, at all costs. To love another is
to invite new kinds of anxiety and new possibilities of
guilt.

I have contended that a person needs a home dedicated
to his growth in value as a person. And I have done so on
the assumption that a person does not grow if he can depend only on a hand-to-mouth existence emotionally and
that he is equally crippled if he is hell-bent to avoid discomfort, uncertainty, and anxiety at any cost. Parents and
children both, in different ways, need to accept all the
responsibilities that go with preparing themselves for what
they profoundly need as persons, namely, responsive-
responsible love.

Therefore, assuming that our children's children ought
to be able to take sex casually and have "sex without
guilt," my basic question is: Would they pay no price for
this supposed freedom? My answer is that they would endanger the experiences of sexuality as a creative source of
unity and community in their lives. Yet my answer is
sorely pressed in the following question.

Why Isn't Sex With Love Enough?

Let us make as strong a case as we can for Andy and Mary (see above, p. 103) who had agreed on limitation of petting in their early adolescence. Suppose now, at the age of 20, they are juniors in college and very much in love with each other, and argue: "We grant you all that you have said about the dangers of sex exploitation. We have in our years together been able to keep our petting meaningful to us. With mutual understanding and help we have been able to refrain from sexual intercourse. But we love each other, and in a year or so we plan to be married. We are in good health; we like the same kinds of friends; and our values are basically in harmony. We believe that if ever two persons could symbolize the unity they feel and celebrate their joy and commitment to each other by the joining of their bodies in sexual intercourse, we can. In other words, if you are saying that committed love, supported by a promising background in harmonious value-experience, is the basic prerequisite for quality of value-experience, we think we meet the conditions. Today, we can prevent pregnancy. Why should we then wait to get married in order to express physically our commitment to each other?"

This question must be taken seriously, so seriously that I wish to interpret it in the light of our whole previous discussion. Let us assume, therefore (what cannot in fact be readily assumed), that before two young people meet, they have made reasonable progress in discovering their own identity. They have enjoyed successful friendships and have prepared themselves for jobs within the scope of their abilities. Yet, like so many young people who are both well-adjusted at home and co-operative members of their peer groups, they still know the loneliness that is inevitable as they try to realize their own value-potential. They wonder whether they will find another who will share their ventures in meaning and value. They yearn for a kind of togetherness that is possible only to persons who are faced with the same basic problems.

Hence, before Andy and Mary know each other, they are ready to be loved and to love in a way that even parental relationships and "very good" friendships could not provide. Then they meet each other; at first, each can hardly believe it possible that there is another person so good, so understanding. As they get to know each other, a togetherness does develop, and their engagement becomes its natural symbol.

Older folk may smile at the language that the young sometimes lavish upon such an experience. I think of the young man who characterized his love as "a life-giving power" and then went on to say: "Where before I was hoping and praying, now I am hopping and praising. I feel our love is creating a union between us, and between us and God." Andy and Mary could go on to say: For us to be in love is for us to *feel* a unity we never experienced in quite this way before; we each *feel* that there is a place in the other's life, central to our being; we already *feel* each other as mates, for better, for worse. No poem, no church, no holy vow can *create* this sense of commitment in us. Remember, our love is not born of lust; it is not born of this desire or that desire. We are not interested simply in conquering, or in possessing, each other![2] We understand Erich Fromm when he says: "Lovers are not victimized by

---

[2] See Alfred Stern on Sartre's view in *Sartre: His Philosophy and Psychoanalysis* (New York: Liberal Arts Press, 1953), p. 126.

passion; they are sustained by purpose. . . .[3] Our deepest need is the need to also overcome our separateness, to leave the prison of our aloneness . . . We want to communicate with each other from the center of our existence."[4]

When one is faced with such a case—and I have heard words like these from many, many young people—he refrains from reminding them that this being "terribly in love" can still be enthusiasm that could be more short-lived than they think. But I prefer to assume that this is not the case and move to my last concern which, I have found, does get a respectful hearing.

For one to *love* another person, for two people to be *in love with each other,* means that they are embarked on a new venture. It is the venture of undergoing *together,* gladly, joyously, nobly, solemnly, the interpenetration of their values. This will take time, work, dedication, patience, imagination. For each person has his unfinished symphony of values; and the problem for each is how to deepen it and enrich it by sharing, as it were, the musical knowledge and the style of the other. The aim is not to produce one symphony, for that is impossible and undesirable; it is to join together in a love of music and of each other's music, the first contributing to the second, the second to the first. This union is not the immersion of one in the other; it is the growing purpose in common that makes also for individual excellence. And this means that they want their affiliation to be a community in responsive and responsible freedom, a community of love.

The point is critical. Love is not like a bank account upon which Andy and Mary can draw as they live together.

[3] Erich Fromm, *The Art of Loving* (New York: Harper, 1956).
[4] *Ibid.*

Of course, there is the deposit of all their being, the sense
of union they both feel in their values and purposes. But
love that is not invested in new undertakings will not grow.
To be "in love," then, must mean a willingness to do all in
one's power to create values in a constantly new relationship.

Furthermore, in every human love there is always a tension owing to the fact that we need to grow as human
beings from childlike dependence to independence, and
then on to dependability. There is always the tension between "I want to be loved" (so characteristic of the dependent person), "I want no strings attached" (so characteristic of the independent person), and "I want to love"
(so characteristic of the creative person). The creative
person is willing to invest himself in a task that challenges
his every power. The supreme test of Andy's marriage with
Mary will consist in love's shift of meaning from "I want
to be loved" to "I want to love," to "I want to keep my
love growing." And, to put it in my imagery, to "want to
love" is to encourage the creation of finer symphonies everywhere and especially in the loved one.

To summarize: Beyond the sexual progression, there is
the progression of love. And this progression is risky because it is creative. One might almost say: "If you want to
learn to love another person, marry him!" But, in the same
breath: "If you want to learn to hate him, marry him."
The surgeon and his wife, to whom we referred in the first
chapter, had experienced love that turned to hate because
that "love" could not take root in enough common values;
it was not invested in new ways of mutual sharing, including a philosophy of home and children. The love of Ann
and Jim (pp. 12–16), rent to its foundations when the
baby died, was a deeper love after their child had died;

Jim, as Ann said, "put me back together again, piece by piece."

What has all this to do with the question: If we love each other, why should we wait until marriage to express our love in sexual intercourse? The answer is in the counter-question: "Do you love each other enough to forego what might indeed be the very meaningful experience of sexual union for the sake of creating the best conditions for its continued creativity in your lives?" What we call "legal" marriage is, at its best, an effort to maintain and protect such conditions once they have been envisioned and established by the community. For example, the law against theft does not merely coerce the would-be thief; it supports the conditions under which ownership of property, public and private, can be fruitful. The good citizen, if he accepts the law, accepts the philosophy in or behind the law. Those who wait to consummate their love after legal marriage have answered "yes" to each other and to the question implied in the law: Do you care enough for each other to promise before all men (and before God, or in the name of whatever sense of integrity you have chosen to live by) to accept full responsibility for the growth of your love? Do you feel sure enough of your love to pledge yourselves publicly to each other as members of the larger community that makes your values possible?

I say this, though I know that the letter can kill while the spirit gives life. Yet even the Word had to be made flesh and be subject to the Law to dwell among men. I know that the ritual of marriage, in itself, has only the power we give it. Rituals and ceremonials can re-enact our inner marriage. They dramatize what our love is aiming at, a new communion in a larger community. The marriage ceremony solemnizes what we feel, imagine, and will by bringing it into symbolic expression. Ritual solemnizes because it reaches out imaginatively toward all the powers upon which a human being depends. Can we afford, as it were, to "cheat" the ceremony that celebrates publicly our completing the preparatory emotional, intellectual, and social cycle that expresses the "all of us" in love? To dramatize one's deepest meanings in one another's presence and before mother, father, family, friends, society, and whatever you may mean by God, is not only to see one's purpose writ large but to impress upon the total personality one of the images that can be a resource in moments of faintness of heart and vision.

Much more is at stake here than the legality of marriage. What is at stake is the aspiration of love to depth and breadth. What the ceremony enacts is the conviction that, come what may, the lovers are committed to each other as persons in every dimension of their being. Their growth as persons will need mutual care and dedication, in illness and in health, if it is to become an experience in which the whole being of each person is satisfied. Sex-values, like other values, must be part of a growing symphony of values. The marriage ceremony, the marriage vow, is the imaginative projection of the ideal purposes of a union not only as it relates to the two principals, but also as it affects the family and the social institutions that have contributed to their love. The marriage ceremony is not just a legalization of a private agreement in the public presence. It is commitment through a symbolic act, which itself can add inestimable efficacy, to the solidarity between individual love and the total community that has nourished it.

Why Sex and Love Need Marriage

In our effort to make Andy and Mary realize that their very sincerity of purpose, in order to be fulfilled, calls for resources that their individualism overlooks, we may seem to have pressed too hard the importance of ritual and ceremony. It is so easy for young people today to think that they are living in a different world or a different age. They trust "reason" manifested in some "psychological discovery" to explain away what seems to be restrictive and not "authentic." They use the same "reason" as a warning against being too reasonable because psychology has "exposed" subrational and nonrational roots of behavior and ritual. They readily become suspicious of all the ancient forms of envisaging the fact that we do not live only by ourselves or unto ourselves. But they seem to forget that they think *it is reasonable* for them to think this way! So I shall not apologize for one last searching look at Andy's and Mary's proposal to live in love through "safe" sexual intercourse until the time comes for marriage.

Evidently, the two young people expect to express their love for each other sexually without binding their lives to each other socially, economically, or legally. That is, they will live as though married without accepting responsibility for each other in the eyes of their fellow men and of the state (at least). They will live as though married without sharing the same living quarters, without needing to work out daily problems that any two married persons have to face as they settle into the tasks of housekeeping and making their way in the community. They will live as though married, but their love will not have been put to work. One can conceive of this situation for the traditional lover and mistress who expect, sooner or later, to part; for two people who plan to marry, it wastes the opportunity of enlisting romance and the power of a new affection on the side of the tasks marriage must perform in their lives.

Marriage will leave few areas of the personality untouched. It will call for constant sharing of satisfactions and disappointments that need to be and can be shared together only if they are living together in marriage. Love in marriage is forced to develop new roots, which take firm grip on the value-soil that nourishes the lovers and reaches out to embrace more and more of their lives as persons. The test of a marriage, like that of a tree, is the power to find nourishment in the soil of the common life and to encompass in its branches ever more fully their ideal aspirations.

These considerations support the conclusion that premarital intercourse, though between pledged lovers, invites even sexual disappointment. It creates an artificial state and isolates sexual experience from the total pattern of their values. When sex is an experience that two people can have in the midst of their other joys and sorrows, it contributes to the ongoing interlocking of both lives and it develops a quality not attainable otherwise. For marriage both encourages and symbolically expresses the growth in unity that the lovers experience in every area of their lives. Sexual intercourse before marriage is no preparation for marriage; it "tests" very little. In a word, a so-called "marital intercourse" withdrawn from the real context of marriage is hardly calculated to keep love honest, let alone growing.

We are not suggesting that Andy and Mary, having been in love for, say, a number of months, cannot possibly find in their first premarital experiences of sexual intercourse a new point of unity for that particular stage in their relationship. This will depend upon their past sexual conditioning, on their capacity to quiet (for good or ill) the scruples that may well beset them in the light of their moral training and sense of social responsibility—in brief, on the content of their consciences at that time. But Andy will do well to bear in mind that, if he does love Mary and wants to help nourish her self-respect and confidence in her capacity for being a good partner, there is danger, as well as a lack of generosity, in the demand for premarital sexual intercourse (see pp. 101–102). For he may be expecting from her more than she can psychologically afford to give, however willing she is to give of herself in the name of love. The same applies to Mary in her relation to Andy.

Furthermore, Andy and Mary, on having normal intercourse, may not enjoy unity of mutual response, either owing to interfering moral scruples or to the difference in responsiveness. Generalizations are dangerous, but is it psychologically far-fetched to urge that a young couple must even in marriage take some pains in working out their responses to each other? If Andy and Mary are married and encounter difficulties in sexual adjustment, the total conditions under which they live will provide both incentive and opportunity to improve their relationship. In addition, marriage provides many ways in which any temporary deficit in sexual mutuality may be made up by either mate.

If, on the other hand, Andy and Mary are unmarried and find their sexual experience less than satisfactory, they are likely to consider it more of a problem. They may hastily conclude that they are not suited to each other. Thus they will have created conditions thanks to which the experience that was to unify them further actually raises problems of its own. If they decide to separate it will not be

because they have "tried marriage." They have in fact
remained in the limbo of marriage.

In sum, the sexual experience deserves every emotional
and circumstantial encouragement it can get if it is to be a
growing experience of enrichment. The tragedy of so
much premarital sexual experience is not that it is premarital, but that it is shockingly disappointing and destroys
confidence. Andy and Mary want to be one. Yet, perhaps
without realizing it, they both actually want a quality of
joy that sexual release itself cannot give; and when they do
not find it, they can be more deeply disappointed than they
are readily willing to admit. What they are likely to neglect
is the all-important fact that, if sexual experience is to be
an increasing source of unity, a bearer of joy and creativity,
the lovers must bring to it the imagination and the discipline that any art demands.

No art is developed without thought, patience, and self-
forgetfulness. Many young people have in principle decided against premarital sexual intercourse and, frankly
facing the difficulty of self-control, have learned to help
each other meet the problem as their courtship developed.
Such young people have not felt that they loved each other
less, and indeed they have come to understand better the
springs of their love for each other. Early in their love-
lives, they have learned to forego immediate self-gratification in the interest of other values. Such knowledge can
be a source of confidence; it can discourage suspicion and
jealousy during stretches of married life when absence or
illness make sexual intercourse impossible.

In order to consider another possibility, however, let us
go so far as to assume that sexual conditioning (the content
of sexual conscience) is such that Andy and Mary can

enjoy a high quality of mutuality even in their early premarital sexual experiences. The question I would now ask is: How long will Andy and Mary continue to keep the experience high in quality, growing in quality, a binding force between them if, unmarried, they are not sharing the other investments in their lives?

I need not urge again that the sexual experience needs favorable conditions if mutuality is to be encouraged. Once the early bloom of a new experience wears off, Andy and Mary may well find it more difficult to maintain the earlier mood and zest, with the result that qualitative decrease sets in. Married persons testify to the fact that it is not a simple matter to be emotionally and otherwise prepared for the fulfillment of sexual experience that is more than sexual release. What will Andy and Mary experience when, unmarried, they find themselves cut off from the other ready sources of mutuality, strength, and growth that will, on the one hand, compensate for less fulfilling sexual experiences and, on the other hand, provide the substance for richer experiences?

The relevance of these considerations came out in a recent conversation with a coed who had married as a sophomore and followed her husband to graduate school. He had earned his advanced degree and had begun to teach at a secondary school. She continued with her education and had "discovered Shakespeare" and the arts. Strangely enough, the discovery had put a strain on their marriage. She put her concerns in words like these: "John and I have been married almost three years now, and I'm getting worried about our marriage. Something seems to be wrong."

When asked whether she thought that their sexual

adjustment was good, she said: "Well, we did have some difficulties in harmonizing our responses to each other in the first year, but we haven't had unusual difficulties, and I don't think the trouble is there."

When pressed further along these lines she said: "Sometimes he says I'm not responsive enough. But how can you really be responsive to a man for whom you are beginning to lose respect? I'm finding it less than easy to respond with all of me to someone who doesn't seem to want to share other parts of my life too. I admit that three years ago I didn't dream that I could go for Shakespeare and for music and painting as I do now. But all he seems to want to do now is teach his class, play bridge, and putter about with boats and cars. He treats me and my interests with surprise and not with inner sympathy. If I mention philosophy or religion he takes the attitude: 'I couldn't care less.' And now I'm discovering that my being attractive and keeping a clean house is part of a general bargain for which he's 'settling.' I don't even have anything to say about the budget."

Here, then, are two young people who fell in love, married, and enjoyed sexual intercourse without qualms or fears. Before three years had passed, even this part of their young lives was beginning to drag. Would it have been better for them to have practiced birth control without marriage for two years? Would they have thus discovered that they were "incompatible sexually"? Would their earlier sexual intercourse have taught them to avoid sexual obstacles in marriage? Hardly. Sex in their lives was feeling the impact of other separations, and she was beginning to feel "divorce." She could still enjoy sexual intercourse at a certain level of her being, but this was not what she wanted any longer. As she said, "I'm not sure I want him to be the father of my children." And he certainly had been going through changes effected by his work and his new experiences.

It would not be true to say simply that they did not have enough in common to begin with. What was happening is nothing new in the experience of married persons. The early months of their marriage over, they both were not so much "settling down" as "settling up" accounts with their immediate past. What they needed, and indeed proceeded to under guidance, was to re-think their value schemes, allow for growth and change, and yet re-affirm on a new level the union they had felt in their early marriage.

How many older married people throughout their married lives know the same thing to happen more than once at different levels of their lives? They are always being unsettled in some way—settling down, settling up. The children are not exactly what they had wished their children to be, their physical health takes different courses, their economic lives and their cultural involvements change—all the things take place that are so wisely called "for better or worse" in the marriage vow! It is married people who can best testify to the different meanings their sexuality takes on as they keep trying to "stay close" to each other, as they find meanings—and meaning—in their lives. For *this* young couple the rift began to appear in *their* lives after two and a half years.

In this instance, fortunately, they were willing to face their emerging problems. They were able to talk to their parents, to their pastor, to a marriage counselor; and because they did take their vow seriously, they gradually developed the roots that made for togetherness in their lives, and they live today in a *home* of their own building with values that allowed for their individuality without separating them. A marriage that could have been deadlocked has now become wedlock on a firmer basis.

Over and over again, one hears young people urge that if they can have "safe" intercourse before they are married, they will be able to get the experience they need and not be naïve in marriage. Older married persons can tell them that there is nothing more naïve than to suppose that earlier "experience" is a good basis for finding the meaning sex can give when, protected by responsible love, it symbolizes the sharing of values and growth in values that persons need in marriage.

No amount of "safe" intercourse, then, before or after marriage can keep sex meaningful at the various stages of life. Crisply put: Why should the rules for sexual success be essentially different from those for other desires? Quality of gratification, or satisfaction, will always be lost where larger meanings cannot be expressed. Sex does not make marriage, and love does not make marriage or even a home. But sex and love both need marriage and the home to challenge, to preserve, to increase their creative power in the lives of persons.

Finally, let us draw a conclusion from our analysis that applies to a question asked by many worried people. What will happen to chastity once contraceptives have removed the fear of pregnancy with its economic and social consequences?

Psychological and moral chastity is not sensitively defined, in the last analysis, in terms of whether a person has or has not had sexual intercourse. Chastity basically consists in the motivation and practice that keeps sex from being self-centered and self-indulgent and that constantly dedicates it to the growth of value. Chastity, if it is worth protecting, must be protected within the marriage bond as well as outside it. That is, neither the husband nor the wife is chaste as long as one uses the other simply or largely as a means of sexual gratification. Sex in itself is prostituted when it becomes a source of self-enslavement and not a growing phase in the total development of mutual concern between two people. As long as chastity stems from fear of progeny and social disgrace alone, the emphasis will tend to be placed on whether sexual intercourse is licit or not, rather than on the conditions that make for quality in and through sexual experience. Thus persons will continue to lose a creative source of goodness in their lives.

The "Home" of Sex, Love, and Marriage

I have argued against premarital sexual intercourse among "lovers" by urging that sex and love alone are the cut flowers of life, which soon die because they have lost the roots that gain nourishment from the good earth. Creativity in the lives of persons is, of course, not restricted to sex, love, and marriage. We all know persons who, whether by circumstances or by choice, have lived full lives without "sex and love" because they have been able to orchestrate their values in other ways that challenge them to self-realization. What these persons show us is that persons can be creative without sex and without marriage, because their love is tied to other goals that give "vocation" to their existence.

My thesis is not that sex is crucial to the development of personality. My thesis is that sex cannot live as a refreshing and creative experience outside of the commitment of love, marriage, and home (and all that a home stands for). There are no short cuts to creativity for either sex or romantic love. Persons cannot live the fragmented lives that sex and love alone involve without finding that the springs of creativity in sex and love are likely to run dry because they do not reach the deeper tributaries provided by the other values in their lives.

I am aware, of course, that special instances may be cited of very creative persons who seem to experience sex and a profound love without marriage and home, but I suggest that if their sex and love is to remain creative they too will have to find what marriage and home can provide in the lives of most human beings. In the meantime, the values they experience would hardly be possible unless others had dedicated their sex and love to the creativity of marriage and home. An adequate substitute is yet to be found for the way in which sex and love can be fused creatively in the vocation of marriage and home as here envisioned. In monogamous marriage two persons are united in a partnership that inspires both growth in individuality and in mutual dedication to common goals. Other loves and other sources of sexual gratification ultimately remain parasitic upon those who have devoted themselves to creative sex and love in a sustaining marriage and the vocation of home.

It would be unfortunate if our discussion should leave the impression, since so much has been said about the conditions for creative love in unmarried young people, that our argument has no special relevance to "married love." Just the opposite is intended. For if the analysis is at all correct, it applies as well to the quality of sex and love among married persons. Indeed, that was the main reason for beginning our discussion, in Chapter 1, with marriage and the home.

Much more attention needs to be given to the problems of married persons as they seek to find meaning for their lives in and through, and beyond, their marriage and families.[5] All too many married persons are not finding in their sexual experience the possible creativity it can contribute to their lives because they too tend to think of it as a fragment of their lives. Their sexual experience easily becomes a routine habit or custom that loses its symbolic expressive value. Because they have allowed the other springs of meaning to become routine, because they have not caught, or have lost, the vision of what a home for themselves, for their children, for the community, and for their God can be, even their love becomes more habit than challenge. They need to be remarried in love, in sex, in their common worship; "divorce" begins to occur when they begin simply to "use" each other for the "conveniences" of married life. Yet their very marriage, their commitments to children and community can be the occasion for new creativity, because it is here that *their* values are tested and put to work. *Their* home changes as their values grow and take them into new realms of growth.

Home, then, is the living atmosphere conducive to human growth. It is always made by a marriage of some kind as the source on which persons, younger and older, can thrive. For here there is dedication to a patience and compassion guided by imagination, to appreciation of goodness never taken for granted, to mutual support sobered by knowledge of weakness and failure, to justice in the service of steadfast love, to a vision of growth that is never sentimental or self-righteous. Men in these days are

[5] See Constance Robinson, *Passion and Marriage* (London: Society for the Promotion of Christian Knowledge Press, 1965).

removing the distances between things, but only the home can remove the distances that separate persons as they develop.

In all that I have said in opposition to plausible new schemes of reorganizing sex relations, I have been concerned with the protection of this creative matrix I have called the home. If these schemes are to be blamed, it is because they promise through sex to lead to a "home" where there is no home. It is not so much that sex, love, and marriage make for a home but rather that the creation of a home brings sex and love to fulfillment, because it unites persons in creative intercourse in every dimension of their beings. "Home," once more, is the name we give to that vital atmosphere in which man seeks to create, in the sympathetic presence and with the co-operation of others, those unfinished symphonies of value that give life its quality and meaning.

In this atmosphere the quality of sexual experience will be kept alive and growing, because here sex is never simply the attempt to grasp temporary gratification in a psychological slum or spiritual vacuum. If our human experience has proved anything, if it does prove anything day by day, it is that the best way to destroy values in our experience is to try to isolate them from the total value-ventures in our lives. Nowhere is this truer than with sex-quality; nowhere is it more tragic than in lives that would protect love by not allowing it to inspire and infuse their total undertakings as human beings. For love is the expression of that yearning for creativity that fulfills itself among persons who seek communion in community.

6 THE HARD QUESTIONS IN BROADER PERSPECTIVE

I have been arguing that the quality of sexual experience and of love depends on the meanings and values that persons bring to them, that sex and romantic love are values that can be appraised only in the context of the total achievement of value in persons and in community. Unfortunately, a great deal of the discussion of the so-called "sexual revolution" has not come to terms with the fundamental question: What kind of persons ought we to become? Somewhere in the discussion there lurk hidden assumptions about what can and ought to be expected of human beings, especially in our day.

The concern in this book has been to become more explicit about the values governing decision, to present an ideal of the person in the light of which we can judge the changes that are said to be taking place and the new considerations that are relevant to sexual morality in our day in particular. Larger ethical issues are involved than we have touched. But, avoiding polemics, I have restricted myself mainly to expounding a perspective, aware that such issues were involved in every topic treated.

In this chapter, therefore, I wish to place some of the persistent questions we have discussed in a larger context. I

135

want to avoid any suggestion that objections to my conclusion are mere rationalizations of strong desires. For, I
would agree, when a person is confronted with a strong
desire that "comes naturally," the burden of proof rests
upon the one who asks for control. In any case, a reconsideration of some of the main questions against a background should serve to clarify both the issues and the basis
for my conclusion.

Petting With Consent—A "Paper-Cup" Morality?

What is the harm in petting, short of sexual intercourse?
I myself cannot answer this question with a simple: This is
the harm! That is the good! I suppose one could say that
there is no harm in touching another person as long as one
does not hurt him—or his sensitivities—and has his or her
permission.

Let us omit the important phrase, "with his or her permission," for a moment, and think of petting as a means of
deriving gratification by caressing or manipulating another body. A little reflection can bring to mind a hundred
reasons for our saying that our bodies are not to be used by
anyone for *his purposes without* our consent. The touching of another body "just because I feel like it," or because
I can overpower it for my purposes and gratification, is
equivalent to treating another body as if it were a thing,
and one's own. Restrictions against such casual "handling"
are implicit in any code of behavior, whether it involves
pushing or jostling another person unnecessarily or the
using of a convict's body as a guinea pig for medical purposes without his consent. Enslaving another person, fight-

ing him, means using another person's body as a mere instrument for one's own needs.

These remarks would be trivial if they did not begin to make the point we shall develop. When a person uses his body, he behaves in a way that expresses some meaning or other in his own life in relation to other persons. A given act must be seen in terms of its meaning for the two persons involved, but bodily interaction for the sake of one's own gratification is *not taken for granted* by any person sensitive to the rights of another human being.

Hence petting behavior (short of sexual intercourse) must be seen in terms of its mutual effect along the whole spectrum of one's being. A kiss may be an act of curiosity, a source of aesthetic delight or disgust, a glad greeting, a perfunctory "lip shake"—or a way of saying "I love you." But it is as natural to resent another person's using one's body as he would a paper cup as it is to enjoy the sensitive expression of good will. A "paper-cup morality" of petting is degrading to either party.

If we now bring back the phrase "with his or her permission," it might indeed seem on the surface that, granted such permission, any basis for offense is removed and that no bad effects will ensue. But this is to forget the facts presented in our account of sexual progression.

Petting both expresses and intensifies sexual emotions and desire, creating the want for further exploration. If the sexual stimulation is left to itself, exploration will seek its climax at the sexual peak, or orgasm.

Of course sexual stimulation cannot be "left to itself" entirely in the life of a person. What we have in mind here is the fact that our sexual drive sets up the conditions for its own gratification. The person who seeks sexual release or reduction of tension has to deal with his own tempo and intensity of response, and this will not remain the same in the progression from "holding hands" to "kissing" to "heavy petting." The point of release moves, and the person finds himself no longer gratified on a given occasion at the stage that had brought gratification earlier. A particular stage of response becomes uninteresting and ungratifying; what is more, the particular person who has been the source of release is no longer interesting or gratifying.

The more the person yields to the rhythm or progression of his own escalating need for sex-pleasure, the quicker and the less considerate do rejections become. The person seeks another kind of response, a different partner or partners—all because the emphasis in sexual responsiveness left to itself is on the mechanical process of self-gratification. The person whose sex education has not included an awareness of this phase of his responsiveness may well find himself moving faster than he had imagined possible to unintended results.

Yet the point to be emphasized is that if the *meaning* of sex for a person *is* sex-gratification, or self-pleasure, the other person functions basically as a mere instrument for his own gratification. The mechanism of appetite and response determines an attitude toward another human being conceived as hardly more than the source of stimulation. While we cannot generalize what exact path will be taken in a specific person, we are simply deceiving ourselves if we think that a person can go on gratifying sex largely for its own sake—"for fun"—without finding himself setting up more problems in his life than reduction of sex-tension. In this situation "fun with"—if all is left to "fun"—becomes fun "at the expense of," and then "no fun," entailing resentment on the parts of both parties.

Hence even if two persons agree to pet, the question

remains: Ought they agree if they do not wish to create such problems for themselves? How many adolescents have discovered themselves escalating to more intimate petting and then to sexual intercourse, their bodies being prepared far in advance of their total emotional and moral sensitivity? If we brush these facts aside—along with all the factors that make it easier to pet and to lose self-control, such as liquor and the unchaperoned party—it cannot be because we really care for the emotional growth of our young people.

Much of the problem in adolescence is to find balance in growth. Young people who are frustrated in other phases of their lives turn to the immediate pleasures for release. But such release can create a new set of problems and frustrations. Often sexual intercourse is the only way out for them because they have not found the other value-resources in themselves for controlling the progression. But often they have not found such value-resources because they lost confidence too early in their own power to deal in more effective ways with frustrations. Seduced by success on the purely mechanical level into thinking that they have solved the major problem of being attractive to the opposite sex, they make a sad discovery. Sex has lost much of its expressive meaning in their lives even though it has increased its power to enslave them. Thus, what may seem to be the simple problem of petting another's body for fun, becomes the horrible realization that sex is no longer a way of "saying something meaningful" to another; it has become a way of conquering another with whom one has been progressively *losing touch* as a human being.

Everything I have been suggesting about petting is equally true about sexual intercourse, for which bodily stimulation is normally the preparation. The essential thesis remains: The use of another person even with consent is wrong, without or within marriage, because under circumstances where no other values sustain the relationship another person is used mainly as a means for one's own gratification. Such practice, furthermore, eventuates in decrease of the value of sex itself as an experience that brings two persons together in mutual appreciation.

It will be noted that I have made no reference to the possibility of unwanted pregnancy or disease. For I am assuming that drugs or contraceptives could be used to obviate such consequences, even though I know that so often the young people "caught" are those who did not intend to go too far and did not take "precautions." The fact remains: Prostitution is the use of another person for one's own convenience even with apparent consent of the other. When one human being consents to, and is willing to, profit by another human being's low valuation of himself, humanity is degraded in both.

More will be said on this matter in the next section. Still it is in this larger context that a person needs to decide about the degree and kind of petting he will allow himself, short of sexual intercourse. Policy will be decided of course by one's assessment of sexual intercourse, but assuming that the latter is not the desired goal, the persons involved will need to be guided by the way in which petting can be a source of value in their lives without endangering other values. And this takes us to the next set of questions.

*Premarital Sex Between Congenial
Partners—A Morality Without Bonds*

But why should young people wait until they are married, or even in love, to have sexual intercourse? As long as both partners are willing, and as long as pregnancy can be avoided, why should they wait? Granted that sex without love and marriage may indeed not be very meaningful, is there any good reason for postponing sexual gratification until marriage, especially if both persons are willing and if no danger to society is involved? Indeed, isn't the whole case based on the questionable, if not false, assumption that it is harmful to have premarital intercourse? Hence, granted that one cannot have caviar at every meal, and that one will have to wait for love, marriage, and home for the best, what is so bad about premarital intercourse with a congenial partner? I raise this set of questions again, even though they have already been answered in principle earlier.

In the first place, let me state my main tenet uncompromisingly. This book would not have been written if the only harm that sexual intercourse could bring to the lives of persons were physiological. While we cannot neglect the fact that there is an increase in venereal disease, that unwanted babies are being born with and without marriage, despite the availability of preventive measures, in principle the problem is not one of undesirable biological consequences. This book is written out of a concern that we consider carefully the conditions under which sex can make its best contribution in human life. The underlying claim is that if persons are casual about sexual experience, if, be it before marriage or within marriage, they use sex as an "outlet," as a kind of cocktail release, sex does not in fact refresh, and more problems are created by such an attitude than are solved. Certainly it does not make for growth in the personality as a whole.

The fact is that despite all our supposed "new knowledge" and all the talk ensuing supposedly from it, the sexual experience even in the lives of many married persons is not the source of creativity it might be once the dynamics of sex, love, marriage, and home are understood and kept in mind. Therefore, the main problem we confront as persons is: How do we keep quality in an area of life which is a source of pleasure and can be a source of creative joy?

The basic answer is that one gets no more out of sex than he brings to it. A person cannot treat sex as a purely biological need without seriously endangering its total value and meaning in his life. To say this is not to assume that some premarital sexual intercourse is sure to maim a life emotionally—though in some instances this may indeed be the case. Nor would I argue that premarital chastity by itself guarantees growth in marriage. Once more, we cannot talk about sex and its place in life in a value-vacuum.

There is no predicting what the effects of one or a series of experiences, at the age of 16, 21, or 45, will be on a life as a whole. Our interest in stressing adequate sex information and education (see Chapter 3) was based on the conviction that it was bad *policy* to leave sex information to the gang and the street, but we know that millions who have had the most questionable sexual information have been able to overcome these handicaps. Fortunately, earlier specific habits and attitudes may be changed, especially as broader shifts occur in the larger pattern of life.

Granting all this, my basic contention is that we do not make our lives symphonic by doing what comes "naturally," and leaving the future to itself. Everything we know about the relation of past experience to our future leaves the burden of proof on those who would claim that since later on we may be able to play life in a new key, it does not matter how and what we play in our youth. Nothing less is at stake than a whole theory of emotional education.

I am discussing *policy* for guiding education rather than suggesting that I know the dire or felicitous consequences that will ensue *in a particular life* if there is premarital sexual intercourse. Here as elsewhere we live by principles that are based on what we have good reason for believing to be the case, and in accordance with which we develop rules and codes adapted to different stages of our development. Our basic principle is that persons, living with each other in different stages of development, and needing each other's support and challenge, ought to treat others as persons with a view to establishing a responsive-responsible community of persons. And we have been suggesting the basic rules in the area of sex that support the realization of this main *principle*.

I will now leave the defense and take the offense. To begin with, I would challenge what is the almost explicit assumption in all these questions: that there is something wrong about expecting an individual to inhibit a strong urge like sex. Since sex-expression can bring pleasure, it is argued that the burden of proof falls on him who challenges sex-expression, especially in a day when contraceptives and miracle drugs can prevent pregnancy and cure disease. Indeed, I have also heard it argued that, having taught adolescents the science of prevention, we might well teach them to learn the art of moderate sex pleasure just as we would do well to teach them to drink moderately and "like gentlemen." After all, it is contended, in some societies such sexual permissiveness is the rule. If we can add to permissiveness the proper education that would keep our children from becoming inhibited, they might be rid of unnecessary anxiety and enjoy sex as their parents, influenced by negative attitudes toward sex, could not.

I am never quite sure how far such persons wish to take their argument. When they are dominated by the conviction that young people, if restricted by society from following natural impulses, become emotionally disturbed, they argue against "artificial restrictions." But it is never clear, as far as I can see, what substitute will take the place of present parental and social expectations. For example, *if* we concluded that we are so confident that sex in itself can be fun, *if* sexual relations are no more likely to interfere with the development of personality than the acquiring of proficiency at tennis or any sport, are we to be as permissive as we are about tennis partners? Or shall we allow sexual adventure alone to be limited only by personal taste and the resistance of those addressed? Having perceived the implicit chaos in philosophies of *laissez-faire* in other areas, shall we make sex relations its cherished preserve and holiday grounds?

But instead of seeking an easy victory by a reduction to the absurd, let me question two assumptions of the proponents of sexual *laissez-faire*. The first is that sex-inhibition is evil in itself and in its consequences. I grant that temptations to sexual expression are not easy to control, but even less easy to contain is the momentum of sexual progression once the sex urge has been unleashed. But if there are dangers of unrestricted freedom, there are also dangers of inhibition arising from psychological problems attendant upon such sexual expression. It is not unrealistic to say that the gratification of the sexual impulse in a growing person can lead to emotional habits, and accompanying physiological habits, of response that do not make the sexual-response by itself easier to produce. My contention is that the person who makes the pleasure of sexual release a goal in itself will find himself not free but more restricted and confined by the habits of response and expectation he has built up. The inhibitions he would now feel are *not imposed upon him by society,* or by mother and father, but by the dynamics of his own psychological and physiological nature. If the dynamics of what I have referred to as the escalation of sexual desire with relative decrease in satisfaction does not describe the actual situation, then I must acknowledge my error at a basic point in the discussion. But if I am substantially correct, then education and formation of an ethical code should be guided by such dynamics.

Second, to this cause and effect in the area of psychological responsiveness must be added another kind of cause and effect in the area of values. The problem of self-discovery and self-identity is one of discovering value-experiences that will be productive and supportive of other value-experiences. Have we not all, as growing persons, found that we are easily misled into attributing to gratifications that are strong, immediate, exciting, and that require relatively small effort, a greater importance than they turn out to possess? Among these, certainly, is gratification of the sexual impulse. Thus the youth who needs to give more attention to other important components in his life *can* find himself caught in a progression so gratifying as to blind him to other values. We need go back no further than Plato and the Greeks to support this observation.

To the objection that the restrictive, "negative" atti-

tudes toward sex have themselves led us to overemphasis
"in our society," we would reply: Why was it, in the first
place, that such "negative" attitudes were taken? Surely,
among the complex causes we must count the fact that the
interferences of early emotional habits with other important factors in development did help to form the inhibitive
attitudes. To oversimplify the reasons for benighted, restrictive attitudes—to dispose of them as mere Puritanism—
smacks more of wish-believe than analytical realism. Those
who hold that our possession today of miracle drugs and
contraceptives has radically altered the personal problem
every individual faces in finding which values to emphasize
now, which to leave for later and better conditions, remind
one of Molière's doctor who covered up misinformation
about the place of the human heart with the bland assurance that *nous avons changé tout cela* ("we have changed
all that"). I, for one, come back to the fact that the
rule or attitude, "sex-to-relieve-tension," or "sex-for-my-
pleasure," encourages neither the sexual freedom a person
will need in marriage nor the pursuit of the many other
facets of value that are open to the adolescent.

I shall be quite explicit about another assumption governing my argument. I hold that the child who does understand what his sexuality can mean in his life is not "de-
prived" by self-restraint. To be human, to be alive as a
person, is to be in conflict. A person is always faced by
choice of alternatives in his own life and in his environment. Tension there always is and will be—and it will not
be diminished for the thoughtful person. We resolve one
tension or conflict and we face another. We relieve one
uncertainty and anxiety and move to another, hopefully at
a higher level, as when the uncertainty and anxiety about
getting into college, or getting married, is supplanted by

that of doing well in college and in marriage. The main problem for any human being is to resolve one set of conflicts in such a way that he does not invite fruitless and needlessly destructive further conflicts. If I eat the wrong thing now I may feel gratified now, only to be ill later and also pay for my error by foregoing eating other things I enjoy for a while. In any choice I deprive myself of something; no choice of any significance is between "black and white"; no important choice leaves me without some frustration.

The specific question then is: If an adolescent, understanding his sexual choices, in principle decides to deny himself "sex-for-pleasure" or "sex-for-release," is he being asked to do something that will exact serious inner conflict or create more difficult choice situations later? The answer to this question, in the light of present knowledge and human experience, is *no*. But of course, as with so many other decisions, results will depend upon the person's knowledge of how *he* can effectively carry it out.

Indeed, in any society, in every human being's life—whether he is married or not—there is always the problem of sexual control at some point. I have indicated above, and in the discussion of the sexual progression, the problems the individual confronts, and I do not wish to minimize the difficulty of control. But it is time to maximize the sense of self-confidence and emotional poise that comes into the life of a person who knows that he can set controls for himself and forego present gratification for the sake of other values.

The difference between "suppressing" sex and "repressing" sex is that in suppression the person faces his impulses and temptations consciously and decides upon the pattern of control he wishes to live by. Repression takes place when the person has disowned his impulse because of some feared or anxiety-producing result and thus tried to act as if sex were no longer a factor in his life. He thus never develops the capacity for, and confidence in, conscious control and, with that deficit, unwittingly is all the more anxious about the impulse's getting control over him. Because the sexual desire cannot be "drowned," because it is persistent in various ways, if the adolescent can learn to suppress it, without self-righteousness and without self-pity, as part of a larger plan for his life, he may indeed find a freedom not known by another adolescent for whom sex-pleasure has become an overriding necessity.

In any case, my main contention is that if a person faces his conflicts knowingly and realistically, and if he has other values that give ongoing meaning to his life, he will not suffer any more from sex-deprivation than he would from depriving himself of other desires. In the case of sex, as of other values, his individual problem is: What pattern of values makes present "sacrifice" desirable?

The case for convenient sex-for-pleasure between congenial partners is not as impregnable, then, as it may seem at first glance. Yet we still have to consider the more formidable, specific question raised by older adolescents and young adults especially, and single persons generally. I have argued that the quality of sexual experience and the contribution it makes to marriage and the home depends on the purposes and values it expresses and symbolizes. Assuming the use of adequate contraceptives, what shall we say to the young adult who finds a willing and suitable partner for pleasing sexual intercourse and sees no apparent reason to forego the values of these experiences? Such intelligent adults can surely be supposed to understand that their mutual sexual enjoyment is intended to satisfy desire and not to express love and to agree that when they cease giving each other enjoyment they are to part "good friends." As one young man put it: "I am looking now for a companion who would agree on a sexual intercourse to be enjoyed only so long as it provides an aesthetic delight for either of us. When the time comes for marriage, I shall broaden the conditions."

I have already dealt with a general possibility of this kind. But the specific issue now at stake is this: Why should such pre-marital experience interfere with later adjustments with the person loved and married? Why can't we later place what we now use for mutual enjoyment (without commitment to more than that) into a larger context of love and marriage as we move on to the admittedly richer experience that marriage and the building of a home encourage? Why should we imagine one would spoil the other or be a bad preparation for the other?

Before answering this objection, I wish to be doubly clear on several points. I am not asserting that premarital abstinence is the sole or even the most important basis for a good marriage, or that premarital intercourse always interferes with marital harmony later. In such complex situations one simply cannot have foreknowledge of all possible circumstances and of the way in which premarital experience will affect the growth of total value in two lives from year to year. I have asserted only that love and marriage grow to the extent that the co-responsive pattern of values two individuals enjoy and seek does enable them to live together as creatively as possible.

I do not deny that two persons who have had premarital sexual experience may grow together in marriage. In their case the total context of their values, into which sexual experience must fit, may make possible a shift to love. I have no desire to fly in the face of experience, for we hardly need statistical evidence to show that many persons get married with weaknesses in different areas of their lives —including the sexual—and still find it possible to rebuild their lives around a new focus.

Further, as I have argued, two persons are not ready for marriage who are not prepared to weave new patterns and find new meanings. On the value-analysis here presupposed, this will call for the kind of love that means forgiveness with a view to sharing weakness and strength as each develops his symphony of values in relation to that of the beloved. In nothing that I have said is there the suggestion that some one emotional habit, predisposition, or value is the be-all and end-all condition for growth in marriage. Every personality is unique, and every particular individual's organization of values is unique, no matter how similar it may also be to that of one's partner. Who will forejudge with any certainty whether a particular couple, given their patterns of habits, values, purposes, will find in their marriage that premarital experience, or lack of it, is *the* condition of success or failure? My earliest example in this book—that of the contrasting experience of two sets of couples—was meant to show that marriage itself could influence and lead to reorganization of pre-existing patterns of values.

Granting all this, what am I to say *as a matter of principle and policy* to the suggestion that premarital sex-expression with limited objectives among young adults is now (given contraceptives) so harmless that only my joy-killing "Puritanism" can explain my objection to it?

In the first place, everything I have said earlier about sex-for-fun is relevant here. Escalation of desire, demand for variety for its own sake, and relative decrease in gratification will be operative.

In the first place, everything I have said earlier about persons, given the complexity of their natures, will be as successful in quarantining the area of their relationship as they think they can. On the one hand, they will wish as complete a mutual sexual response as possible; on the other hand, they are required to avoid any other significant commitments and check any tendency to take each other too seriously, beyond the area of sexual reciprocity.

Little do they know what they are asking of themselves! Why not frankly face the actual probability—that for the sake of sexual "partnership" they are willing to take all the other risks of hurting each other. On what grounds can they really expect a continuing experience of sexual quality—one island of glowing sexual experience!—separated from the mainland of each of their lives?

In other words, the person contemplating premarital sexual intercourse might well, in all candor, ask himself some questions. What is my underlying aim in seeking a zone of sexual enjoyment detached from other commitments? Am I exaggerating the possibility of such zoning or "unattachment" in my partner's life as well as in my own? Am I rationalizing self-absorption by saying that I am not hurting my partner, who "after all, is a free agent," and presumably knows the score? Does my attitude really amount to a demand upon my partner for a sexual gratification free of any other claims explicit or implicit?

But let us raise the bar a notch to a more fundamental question. Let us assume that a person is able to find a convenient partner of the type described, or a series of such partners. On what grounds does he expect to make an untroubled shift from sex-as-fun to sex as a means of expressing love in marriage? Does he expect the particular habits of emotional and bodily response which now regulate his sexual responsiveness to be easily transformed and to harmonize with the emotional and physical habits and expectations of his partner-in-love?

My own answer to these questions is influenced by such considerations as Dr. Mary Calderone had in mind in a discussion with college women:

> In the repeated sexual act within marriage, a man and a woman are saying to each other, "I choose you once above all others, and I choose you again. I'll choose you tomorrow and the next year and the year after that and when we're 40 or 50 or 60 and neither of us is any longer so attractive." Outside of marriage, the sex act may mean this for a while, but it cannot continue to mean it indefinitely . . . only within the self-sought marriage bond can two people create for themselves the security of peace and solitude and time—lifetime—by which they can accomplish that which is pivotal and central to all else—namely total communion.[1]

Again, I do not wish to pontificate on the preconditions for giving sexual experience a good start in the first days and weeks of marriage. But concern for one's partner's satisfaction, a concern that helps to override one's own rhythm and tempo of response, a concern not only for the present but for tomorrow and tomorrow, a concern expressive of the tenderness and depth of love, will be critical. Yet this kind of concern has the opposite focus from that favored by sex partners who do not wish to be really involved in all of each other's being and becoming. On what experiential grounds can we, with reasonable assurance, say that if a

[1] "The Case for Chastity," in *Sex in America*, ed. H. A. Grunwald (New York: Bantam Books, 1964), pp. 145-146.

person sows experiences basically of self-love he will prepare himself for self-giving and forgiving love? Perhaps in
the concern to deal directly with the sexual need we have
lost sight of the fundamental point—that the person who
makes so big an issue of self-gratification may be the very
one incapable of, or rendered incapable for, the transition
to love and marriage.

Both in marriage and out of marriage persons may think
they can find a togetherness through sex which is not the
kind they seek. Sex can become rather dull routine even in
marriage when married partners forget that sex has been
most meaningful to them when they felt close to each
other in many other ways.

To put it bluntly, be it in or outside of marriage the
unity and community that persons seek cannot be achieved
at the pelvic level—whatever the techniques and acces-
sories! Marriage increases opportunities for sexual experience that can express mutual needs and aspirations, but
not for persons absorbed only in the calculus of their own
pleasure. There is an analogy between those who merely
"hold down a job" and some married people. In business
or in marriage it is better to prepare for a vocation that
will both satisfy needs for living and provide something to
live with. Any marriage raises enough problems of its own,
including those created by temporary or more enduring
changes in sexual desire and expression. It is wiser to enter
marriage without rigidities caused by an experience it
would be hard to defend even to a supposedly liberal-
minded partner. I have a suspicion that those who would
solve problems connected with sex by a policy of *laissez-
faire* are too innocent of a sense of the problems their
remedy would, in turn, bring to the fore.

Hence I come back to the stress laid by Dr. Mary

Calderone, herself a mother with the broader professional experience as a doctor and as Acting Executive Director of the Sex Information and Education Council of the United States:

> The most delicate and the most critical element of a deep relationship is trust, and there is absolutely no way of arriving at trust overnight, for it can be tested only by common experience, and once more—time. Thus it is obvious that there are no short cuts to any true relationship. This leads to the conclusion, by those thoughtful adults in our culture who have been forced to watch sadly and helplessly while young people try these short cuts, that sex experience *before* confidentiality, empathy and trust have been established can hinder, and may actually destroy, the possibility of a solid, permanent relationship.[2]

I return to the fundamental consideration that seems to me has been overlooked in so much talk about the desirability of permissiveness regarding premarital sexual experience. The advent of contraceptives has led us to suppose that sex could somehow be an isolated, or freewheeling, part of a person's life. But the network of consequences involves and goes beyond the biological. One does not do full justice to sex by isolating it or making it tangential. To do so is to negate the original insight into the importance of sex. We do not provide for a child's growth by isolating him from the rest of the family.

Clearly, my argument here is based on certain earlier assumptions—which I have tried to show are not contrary to our human experience—about sex and about love and

---

[2] *Ibid.*, p. 144.

about marriage and about the home. I can only make them explicit in a situation in which no one knows *for sure* what the minimal or maximum meaning of sex in life is, once we have gotten beyond physiology. Here again I take my stand with those who like Dr. Calderone would say: "No one knows what effect sex, precociously experienced, will have on the immature psyche."[3] And I also would urge: "Make no mistake, there is absolutely no possibility of having a sexual relationship without irrevocably meshing a portion of your two nonphysical selves . . . How many times, and how casually, are you willing to invest a portion of your total self, and to be the custodian of a like investment from the other person without the sureness of knowing that these investments are being made for keeps?"[4]

To the persons who claim that they can find "in good clean fun" sexual joy and meaning, "aesthetic delight" as they call it, though oblivious to the demands of aesthetic form for a nonshifting frame—to the persons who say they can find deep meaning in the sex-love experience that means "I promise you, even if we are not married"—I would suggest that everything depends on the *quality* one wants to protect now and in marriage. That quality and its value has its roots in humanity: it is not the withered flower of a puritanical imagination.

I even dislike to overemphasize the "lasting" danger of premarital sex because I wish to avoid creating the unfortunate impression that premarital sex means "it's all over." But neither can I be so anxious lest I create "guilt" about "precocious" adolescent experimentation, or about "responsive" premarital sex that I can say, with what might seem a "sporty" good-humor: "Just check it up to experi-

3 *Ibid.,* p. 143.
4 *Ibid.,* p. 147.

ence." There are experiences that maim, if not ourselves, our partners, and that should not be taken lightheartedly. I am not anxious about creating anxiety; I am only anxious as to what I'm creating anxiety about. For my concern is that sex and love be creative and increasingly expressive of more than a specious sentimentality.

At the same time, it is my concern to give the rationale of *policy* rather than settle once and for all what *may* be the basis for growth in a particular situation. One does not encourage persons to put their fingers in the fire for the sake of warmth, when he sees what it has done and can do to the fingers *and* the person who has been burnt. But it is also no doubt sometimes the case that persons who are burnt by the flames *may*, with proper help, as ministered especially by a loving, committed partner, gain more respect and appreciation for both warmth and flame.

The reflections I have been advancing receive interesting confirmation by the existential psychiatrist Rollo May (who is on the staff of the William Alanson White Institute of Psychiatry, Psychoanalysis, and Psychology). Dr. May sees the fundamental problems in "Puritanism," be it the "old" or the "new," as the attempt to separate the actions of the body from the whole person, the attempt to use the body as a mechanism for gratification but not for complete commitment. *"The Victorian person sought to have love without falling into sex; the modern person seeks to have sex without falling into love."*[5]

This article as a whole, justifies, I think, the view ad-

---

[5] "Antidotes for the New Puritanism," *Saturday Review* (March, 1966), p. 19. Italics his. (This article will appear in a forthcoming book, *Love and Will*, to be published by W. W. Norton & Co. Used by permission of the publisher.)

vanced on page 147, that to *repress* sex is to keep it from relating itself to the whole life of a person. A human being may accept his sexual nature; or he may *suppress* sexual expression not because he is afraid of sex but because he cannot find an adequate place for it in his life. In so doing he will face difficulties, as he will in other purposeful choices he makes. But in suppression he will not suffer from the damaging anxiety that ensues when he never can either deny it or fulfill it; in suppression he can develop confidence in his capacity to cope with his sexual urge. "Our patients," continues Dr. May, "often have problems of impotence or frigidity, but they struggle desperately not to let anyone know they *don't* feel sexually. The Victorian nice man or woman was guilty if he or she did perform sexually; now we are guilty if we *don't*."[6]

The problem in any society—and I join others in raising it—is: "What shall we be anxious about?" If we expect sexual performance with "neat" technique, we "create" anxiety in those who feel frustrated because they can't do what is supposed to come naturally. Hence—we develop the "new sophisticate" who is still a repressed "Puritan." "Sex and body are for him not something *to be* and *live out*," for sex becomes a technique of getting power without real passion or compassion. It loses authentic vitality because it is disconnected with the whole of his life and purpose. The new sophisticate is a "sexual athlete" who is forever worrying about his performance as a sex-partner. He never seems to realize that he cannot keep sex fresh and new because he does not have an enduring partnership in love but only a series of conquests. No one can treat sex and love "like a combination of learning to play tennis

[6] *Ibid.*, p. 19.

and buying life insurance" without banalizing sex and love.[7]

The fundamental mistake in both the Old and the New Puritanism is to minimize the fact that the sexual urge for release can enslave the rest of one's potential for creativity unless it is patiently harmonized, in its individual quality, into a total pattern of life. Sexual athletes will play by the rules of the game, but each with an eye to victory. We still have *l'égoïsme à deux*. Whereas in a finer kind of sexual intercourse, "the lover often does not know whether a particular sensation of delight is felt by him or by his loved one—and it doesn't make any difference anyway."[8]

What Dr. May is clearly stressing is the fundamental human need to overcome alienation and to feel oneself growing in a larger relationship that is never complete but always gives significance to our lives. For as persons we are in our very natures significant because we are significant for and to each other's needs and values. And our values never simply mark time, especially when we vibrate to values of another whose aims become part of our meaning together. At any stage the unfinished "symphony" of our values is one with our own lives as they reach for deeper and broader fulfillment in work, in fellowship, in worship.

"Marriage-in-Spirit"—A Short-Circuited Morality

We must face a final question in our policy-restriction of sexual love to marriage and at the same time be adequately

[7] *Ibid.,* p. 21.
[8] *Ibid.,* p. 43.

sensitive to the dynamic of lovers, especially in this age of the pill. "Your position," it will be said, "seems so arbitrary at this point. For if the pill can keep two persons whose 'engagement' really is a marriage-in-spirit from unwanted pregnancy, why split hairs and become legalistic and argue that they should be married before consummating their love? For surely a marriage in church and under the auspices of society cannot justify their love and make it any holier? Why inflict unnecessary frustrations and possible anxiety upon couples in love who cannot marry (yet or at all). Love cannot and should not be dictated to by social demands; and Christian love in particular must put persons before rules."

Love must indeed put persons before rules—and *all* of the person before rules. If our analysis is correct, it is the person and his growth as a total person that is governing the decision to confine sexual intercourse as love to marriage. For marriage is not something imposed by God or "society" simply to maintain order, "come what may" to persons. To be sure there have been, and there are still, many other reasons for legal and religious marriage; but I shall not advance these here. No responsible thinker is suggesting that we do away with marriage, however necessary it may seem to change the rules for marriage, divorce, care of children, and stewardship of property. The question at issue is whether one of the basic expectations and rules, the confining of sexual intercourse to marriage, has not now lost its relevance, especially for those whose love is so deep that it seems cruel to ask them to postpone full expression for marriage.

And my own considered answer is that if we are to protect the growth of sex and love, then reasonable policy demands of ourselves and our children the expression of

sex within the system of monogamy as the best way of
encouraging creativity in sex and love. For while marriage
does have other reasons, the reason within all reasons is
that persons need each other in a married state because
they love each other as creators of value. Love for another
that excludes concern for his other values—friends, family,
social institutions—is love that has lost its savor and has
degenerated into self-pity and sentimentality.

To love is to be responsive to, and to become responsible for, all that will help the other person, and the other
persons he needs and who need him, to grow. What we
confront is never simply a person but the values in him
and other persons that have gone into making him the
person he is. The situation he is in and each of us is in, as
we indicated above, is never one in which rules are "simply imposed" upon us. What the marriage situation requires is an answer to the question· Can two persons,
granted their present passion and compassion for each
other, find outside of the marriage system any pattern of
action that will give better support to the very meaning
and intent of their love for themselves and for others? We
must not neglect, among our many modern scepticisms, an
ancient scepticism concerning love without system, love as
a way of living that short-cuts self-discipline presumably
for the sake of further growth. Love cannot stay alive and
grow without developing more roots in the lives of the
partners and of their community. Even the pill judiciously
used cannot prevent our love-game from being a dangerous diversion outside the bounds of that system of personal
commitments that alone can keep two people engaged in
exploring mutual values—in themselves as the centers of a
home and in a social order that needs their creative control.

Every system for interpersonal living will inevitably seem rigid and frustrating for young people who have had no direct part in framing it. But nature does not ask for the permission even of the young, nor do the conditions of their growth. A generation that prides itself on facing unpalatable facts should be encouraged to face this particular fact. Let us explain sympathetically, but not capitulate, even for the sake of youth, without confronting the difficulties of our human situation. We have urged that adequate sex education can remove the causes of much unnecessary frustration and anxiety. Yet our emotions are always surprising us, be we young or old. The best we can do is to increase our insight into the ways in which they develop and interpenetrate. Then, far from repressing them because of fears and anxieties that are unjustified, we can suppress them in accordance with the policies and purposes we develop. No system of values, purposes, or policies will work with mechanical ease, for each of us is made to be a unique, changing person, and we grow at different rates and in different ways. Frustrations and anxiety are inevitably so a part of life that our choice can lie only between patterns of life in each of which some frustration is involved. But we can decide, in view of the richest possibilities, in what direction we will confront anxiety. In the area of our sexual lives we can endure the very frustration of immediate expression intensified by love itself for the sake of a richer pattern of life irradiated by that very love.

I conclude, then, that in a total balance of all the values at stake, sexual frustration is tolerable, be it before or after marriage. For marriage is not an easy answer, given once-for-all, to the problem of sexual expression. If sex is to play a continuing creative role in our lives it needs the continuing support of our whole being. I would not take the "fun" or the "humor" out of life. I could even argue that some dreadful pictures of the evils of repressed sex lack a sense of humor. But sex is to be taken seriously because persons, however fallible, are to be taken seriously.

Above all we must beware of oversimplification. We are not simply biological creatures who can live and find fulfillment in biological sex. We are not simply emotional creatures whose passions fret or strut for an hour upon the stage of life and then are heard no more. The ideal poet creates himself through his poetry, the ideal actor through his acting. We are the dramatists, the producers, directors, and the actors of a play that makes us persons with an obligation to treat others as persons. If the plot or plan is shallow, we have a sense of "merely going through the motions." Nor shall we be satisfied with a variety of trivial skits to expend our energies and consume our hours. Why? Because we are persons, with a range and depth of value-experience of which no other creature is capable. Because we are persons whose very loyalty to their own fullest possibility is implicated in a sensitive regard for the possibility of growth in others. To be one's brother's keeper has its dangers for all except the pure in heart; to refuse to do so encourages a moral *laissez-faire* in which indifference to others disguises itself as a concern for their liberty. Our symphonies of value will always remain unfinished, but there can be no symphony at all except through anticipation, in the present, of a future and the coordination of the part with the whole.

Love—Creative Communion in Community

A symphony is a complex musical form which, as such, demands unerring and untiring selectivity even in the liberation of a certain flow of music. The symphony of values, too, requires a tough-minded pruning in order to shape and also release moral forces. It is cruelly sentimental to encourage the notion that a person can live without conflict and the frustration of some desire or set of desires. As a matter of fact, no one is more beset by anxiety than the man who has not learned to live with his frustrations as he works to adapt them to the richest possible harmony of his whole nature.

We make no plea for arbitrary frustration as the source of creativity. The contraceptive pill may remove an external obstacle, but in removing it a new pressure is placed upon the internal resources of form. Love is more creative than sex because it involves the person challenged in weaving that pattern of values together which will keep his own values responsive to his own potential and to that of his beloved. Creativity in love is responsibility for the richest possibility of form.

If intense sexual feeling does not fulfill the demands of love, neither can marriage itself be considered as a mere addendum to love. A marriage is made and not contracted either before the justice of the peace or before the altar. Real marriage comes to be as love realizes it can grow in responsiveness and responsibility through a mutual commitment and a trust more intimate than any other human relationship. Marriage is the form love takes as it fulfills its human possibilities. The marriage vow enacts the drama of faith in a potential unity of form, but the poem must be worked out. The process by which a real marriage is made at the same time creates a home. Love, as we see it, marriage, home—these are a symphony, or any other name one may wish to apply to the same growing reality.

In the home, which is love writ large, the tensions and victories (and even the partial defeats) of love are to be accepted as part of a living process. The home must indeed be a sanctuary in which fatigue, disappointment, and discouragement will meet with understanding and compassion. But in the home new shapings of purpose adjust to the daily successes and failures of each member. A home is not merely a place where, when one fails, they have to take him in; it is the place where readjustment and clearer insight can occur with a minimum of hurt. It is in the very nature of the home, which started in a marriage that respected the demands of the fullest partnership, to adapt itself to new possibilities of growth for the life born of the human pair.

It is to protect the home and its ideal possibilities, to relate the force, yes, even the inspiration or charisma of sexual love from the very first to the social form which is its most "natural" outcome, that I have urged postponement until marriage of sex as the expression of love. I trust that I have not seemed to make this demand arbitrarily and with no sense of the sacrifice involved. And I shall consider one more case in its easier and in its harder form.

The less difficult problem occurs when two young people, hardly 20 years old, whose sense of unity seems to demand consummation in the sexual act, justify intercourse outside of marriage by alleging financial and other difficulties. As one listens to them sympathetically, one cannot help reflecting that if these young people were only more aware of the pitfalls of their easy expectations of love, they might prefer to pay the cost in financial and social sacrifice. Sex can throw its glamor so bewitchingly over what is really the path of least resistance! It may be one of the peculiarities of an age so distrustful of ancient solutions it calls conventional that it looks with so little suspicion on its "liberated" appetites.

The more difficult case is one in which marriage must of necessity be deferred for a year or two at least. One of the young people is a student, perhaps, working for an advanced degree and hardly able to support himself. He may object on principle to support by the young woman who becomes his wife; or there might be other sufficient reasons for her inability to be the breadwinner. How direct and "rational" the solution would seem that consummated their love outside of marriage! Each partner would be indignant at any idea that before the two years were up, one partner or the other might face marriage with less enthusiasm or *élan*. At the present height of idealistic fervor, one or both might even aver that, should they feel less devotion as the time for marriage came, the experiment would be the better justified. Better to have loved and lost the marriage than never to have tested their love relationship.

One cannot help being moved by the spirit of such "idealism." But it is oblivious to a fact of life that we have emphasized repeatedly: that love cannot be set apart from the other relations of everyday life. The proverbial "blindness" of love points, after all, to the refusal of the lover to see his love and his beloved from any other point of view than that of ecstatic isolation. The passionate lover may count the world well lost, for as a matter of fact he has lost the world of relations. But the young people of our case do not belong, presumably, to this category. They do not mean to renounce the world or deny the importance, even the necessity, of relations. They believe they have found the new way—thanks to the alchemy of the contraceptive pill—to have their love immediately, and the world, too!

What they forget, perhaps, is that the "first fine careless rapture" of love, as of inspiration, is given as the stimulus to making a form for its development and preservation. They will meet for sex, then go their separate ways, their thoughts on other things, other friends, other activities. Meanwhile life weaves inexorably its web of relations to which their love remains external. Perhaps for this very reason it seems a privileged and a special thing. Meanwhile they are sacrificing the opportunity to knead the leaven of their sexual feeling into the bread of everyday life by which they must live, after all, once they are married. Nor can its power endure unless transformed into the inter-meshing activities of life as a whole. Such young people are consummating their love when their opportunity for growth together is severely restricted if not cut off.

It is well known that the earlier days of mutual adjust-ment for fully satisfying sexual intercourse may be difficult even in marriage. This young couple, not because they are "unmarried legally," but because they do not have the other rewarding and unifying experiences that legal mar-riage affords, may well find themselves making more of these and other difficulties than they should. In a word, their premarital intercourse will in itself not be the unity they really need as lovers; and they may well find it a more disturbing factor than anticipated. Sexual intercourse, at its best, cannot carry the burden placed upon it by lovers whose other sources of unity are not increased.

But these particular arguments will be less than reasonable to those who cannot accept the idea that unifies our whole discussion. The immediate value in its intensity is likely to take the eye off the total environment on which it depends. Nevertheless, I insist that for persons to love is for persons to be responsible for the most inclusive choice of values possible for them as members of a larger community of persons. To live is to be in conflict and frustration, including those conflicts which love itself sets up as it "seeketh not its own."

Whatever else we do as persons, we realize the constant temptation to use other people to get what we want without adequate concern for their changing and growing needs and values. Each of us as persons is tempted to neglect what the larger community has in fact done for us, whether we deserved it or not. To suppose that it will or should not make hard-to-accept demands, or that it should gladly make exceptions in our own case, is simply saying that we are willing to be parasitic upon that community. And it means to be parasitic at the very point where we can hurt ourselves and the community most, namely, at the point where we can do all in our power to ensure that *we can love and understand,* and not merely *be loved and be understood.* The community cannot encourage persons to take steps that may cripple their capacity to grow in love. There is no loving, there is no home, there is no community that can survive a constant unwillingness to accept sacrifices for the sake of the next step in growth for that partnership, for that home, for that community.

To put this in another way: to love another is to love him *in principle* as well as in fact, that is, to "put up with" this or that annoyance for the sake of the larger co-operation that one does approve. To build a home is to live together for the sake of as much common growth as possible. Children accept father's authority, even though they do not agree with every wish, out of their respect for his concerns and responsibilities. Parents accept what might seem as insubordination from the children to make sure that their own demands are not based merely on arbitrary authority. On principle, then, we expect to demand of ourselves inconveniences and frustrations that will nourish the total morale. On principle, then, we are ready to accept what may seem on the surface to be arbitrary and needless sacrifices. There is no love, no marriage, no home, no community, without a common gratitude and loyalty in the midst of personal hardship.

Having said this, I recognize that there are cases so deserving of special consideration that some of the most sensitive minds among us would ask for a reconsideration of the stand on extra-marital sexual intercourse. I mention one final case out of many I know personally.

A 28-year-old mother of three children, warm, outgoing, dedicated to her children, is alone and will probably be alone for an indefinite future owing to the fact that her husband, a war-veteran, has developed a mental illness that is expected to resist treatment for an indefinite future. Three years of confinement have already passed, the prognosis for her husband is still poor, and she has continued her college work with a view to improving her own future as a person and as a mother. Divorce is not possible for her legally; nor is it acceptable to her for a variety of good "family" reasons. She develops a strong friendship for an unmarried man who would be willing to marry her. "I'm not sure that I do love him enough to marry him even if I were free. But with the contraception now possible, why should I be expected to forego what I believe would be good sexual experiences for us?"

Let me make this situation more difficult by making her friend another man whose own situation prohibited divorce. The point is: Should she be expected to go through life without sexual experience when she could have sexual intercourse, without fear of pregnancy, with a very friendly adult in similar personal circumstances? Does "for better or for worse until death do us part" not become irrelevant in her situation?

To generalize: Am I willing as a matter of policy to require continence from persons whose situation is such that marriage is very undesirable or for whom it is out of the question?

Unhesitatingly I would say yes, in spite of my sympathy for those of whom the sacrifice is demanded. Yes, in principle! Why? If what I have called the *progression of love* is true, such persons are not likely to be able to share in each other's lives enough to make sexual experience itself more meaningful. They will probably avoid frustration at one level only to invite it at a deeper level. The answer is clear in principle; and this means that the expectation is the same for all.

But does this mean that in dealing with a specific situation, it might not be actually a better solution, albeit an unfortunate one, for sexual intercourse to take place than not? I can conceive of circumstances in which it might indeed be better, if the possibility of growth in other respects is to be possible, to accept the breakdown that has led to this risky alternative. Remove one eye rather than lose both—this analogy is not carelessly or casually suggested. But let us live in the understanding that two-eyed vision gives depth! Most of us believe in peace in principle, but we accept war and its unfortunate sacrifices and misery because we have allowed ourselves to reach the point of war, and now hope to save as much as we can in an undesirable situation.

In other words, we need not move from *principles* for the good of persons-in-community as a whole to acceptance, or condemnation, of particular acts *once and for all.* Exceptions do not make the rule; they show us how important the rule is, and they force us to think about any one principle in its relation to other principles. To act "by principle" does not mean to act by one principle alone. Principles grow out of human experience of value, and they are always to be related to the community-growth of persons. To break with a rule in a given case for the sake of improving the situation on the whole is not to become a relativist who denies that there are any guiding principles.[9] Our principles are statements of the directions that we think are best for ourselves and our children; they are never Procrustean beds upon which to lay personalities that would not be helped by amputation. At every stage of our development as persons, nothing can take the place of wisdom in the art of living with our principles.

Throughout this book our goal has been to develop policy in accordance with what seems to be our best experience in sex, love, marriage, the home, and the community of persons. The dominant question has been, and still is: Can we discover a better rule for growth of sexual meaning than control of sex by the kind of love that can create a home?

[9] This is a large question and one dealt with more completely in P. A. Bertocci and R. M. Millard, *Personality and the Good* (New York: McKay, 1963), Chapters 18-27.

SELECTED BIBLIOGRAPHY

Bailey, Derrick S. *Sexual Ethics,* New York: Macmillan, 1963.

Bailey, Sherwin. *Common Sense About Sexual Ethics,* London: Macmillan, 1962.

Bertocci, Peter A. *The Human Venture in Sex, Love, and Marriage,* New York: Association Press, 1949.

————. *Religion as Creative Insecurity,* New York: Association Press, 1958.

Bertocci, Peter A. and Richard M. Millard. *Personality and the Good,* New York: McKay, 1963.

British Council of Churches. *Sex and Morality* (A Report to the British Council of Churches), SCA Press: 1966. American Edition, Philadelphia: Fortress Press, 1966.

Cole, William Graham. *Sex and Love in the Bible,* New York: Association Press, 1959.

————. *Sex in Christianity and Psychoanalysis,* New York: Oxford University Press, 1955.

Committee on the College Student of the Group for the Advancement of Psychiatry. *Sex and the College Student,* New York: Atheneum, 1965.

Cox, Harvey. "Evangelical Ethics and the Ideal Chastity," *Christianity and Crisis,* Vol. 24, November 7, 1964, pp. 75-80.

Demant, V. A. *Christian Sex Ethics,* New York: Harper & Row, 1964.

Doniger, Simon (ed.) *Sex and Religion Today,* New York: Association Press, 1953.

Duvall, Evelyn M. *Facts of Life and Love for Teen-Agers,* New York: Association Press, 1956.

Ehrmann, Winston W. *Premarital Dating Behavior,* New York: Henry Holt, 1959.

Ellis, Albert. *Sex Without Guilt,* New York: Lyle Stuart, 1958.

Fletcher, Joseph. *Situation Ethics,* Philadelphia: Westminster Press, 1966.

Frankena, William K. "Love and Principle in Christian Ethics," *Faith and Philosophy,* ed. by A. Plantinga, Grand Rapids, Michigan: William B. Eerdmans Publishing Company, 1964.

Fromm, Erich. *The Art of Loving,* New York: Harper, 1957.

Grunwald, Henry A. (ed.) *Sex in America,* New York: Bantam Books, 1964.

Havemann, Ernest. *Men, Women, and Marriage,* New York: Doubleday, 1962.

Hefner, Hugh M. *The Playboy Philosophy,* Chicago: HMH Publishing Company, 1962-65.

Heron, Alastair (ed.) *Towards a Quaker View of Sex,* London: Friends Home Service Committee, 1963.

Hettlinger, Richard F. *Living With Sex: The Student's Dilemma,* New York: The Seabury Press, 1966.

Hiltner, Seward. *Sex Ethics and the Kinsey Reports,* New York: Association Press, 1953.

————. *Sex and the Christian Life,* New York: Association Press, 1957.

Kirkendall, Lester A. *Premarital Intercourse and Interpersonal Relationships,* New York: Julian Press, 1961.

————. *Sex Education* (Siecus Discussion Guide No. 1), New York: (1855 Broadway, 10023), 1965.

Kronhausen, Phyllis and Eberhard. *Sex Histories of American College Men,* New York: Ballantine Books, 1960.

Lehmann, Paul. *Ethics in a Christian Context,* New York: Harper & Row, 1963.

Lewin, S. A. and John Gilmore. *Sex Without Fear,* New York: Medical Research Press, 1950, rev. 1962.

Lewis, C. S. *The Four Loves,* New York: Harcourt, Brace and World, 1960.

May, Rollo. "Antidotes for the New Puritanism," *The Saturday Review,* March 26, 1966.

Novak, Michael (ed.) *The Experience of Marriage,* New York: Macmillan, 1964.

Ramsey, Paul. *Deeds and Rules in Christian Ethics* (Scottish Journal of Theology Occasional Papers, No. 11), London: Oliver and Boyd, 1965.

"Religion and the New Morality," *Playboy,* June 1967, pp. 57-80.

Ricoeur, Paul. "Wonder, Eroticism, and Enigma," in Vol. 14, *Cross Currents,* Spring, 1964. (A number devoted to a Symposium on Sexuality and the Modern World.)

Robinson, Constance. *Passion and Marriage,* London: S.P.C.K., 1965.

Robinson, J. A. T. *Christian Morals Today,* Philadelphia: Westminster Press, 1964.

Schur, Edwin M. (ed.) *The Family and the Sexual Revolution,* Bloomington: Indiana University Press, 1964.

Wolfender, Sir John. The Wolfender Report: Report of the Committee on Homosexual Offenses and Prostitution, New York: Stein and Day, Inc., 1963.

Wylie, William P. *Human Nature and Christian Marriage,* New York: Association Press, 1958.